NEW DIMENSIONS

AN ANTHOLOGY OF MODERN POETRY

Edited by

H. M. ROSENBERG

Idlewild

IDLEWILD PUBLISHING COMPANY
543 FREDERICK STREET
SAN FRANCISCO, CALIFORNIA

Only one thing to me is important:
That there be poets,
Many excellent, different poets!
　　　— Vladimir Mayakovsky

INDEX TO AUTHORS

WILLIAM AGUIAR

SANTA CLARA VALLEY

Santa Clara Valley
wonderland of trees
far away from New York
but its the same
exploited, robbed, cheated.

Bean pickers, pear pickers
makebelieve of romance in the
knowledge of $3.56 a day,
surrounded by drunks,
the forgotten,
the left-overs
and a few happy ones.

We are pictures painted by Picasso
picking little green things,
speaking Spanish
and saying prayers for
Luther Burbank.

RUSSIAN FUNERAL

Candles and singing and crying
and prayers from people who
can't always kneel down and
more crying and the smell of flowers
and more prayers.

Embraces and greetings and
tears. More prayers and smiles
and old people whose hands shake
in ritual expressions no one
understands. Dominant chords sing
of death's reward.

Motion slow and almost heavy. The
procession through damp grass and
soft moods. Prayers and singing,
tears and lost flowers. No flowers.

Cement block lowered into place,
no more crying, no more prayers
only invitations to a Russian wake
so that memories of candles and
singing and prayers can be forgotten.

1

INTERMISSION

An opera in San Francisco
is a cape left over
from
romance, tradition
and ethnic promises
that became
slightly polluted
with extra strong
Anglo-Saxon mentality
morality
economic support
and the cape
got
washed "good and clean"
in the sexless innocences
of the
new morality
and the
Bank of America
and now
the music is there
but
the notes
are missing
not even the smell
of garlic
remains

OINK POEM

Rainy twilight/dreams
New York night
streets filled with left-over
junk/still warm from the
kisses of owner's goodbys
bureau drawers and cockroaches
mirrors cracked and sad
chairs still noble in the grandeur
of faded red
dig
find
seek
unscrew
Rainy twilight city
New York lights

2

junk stuffed with memories
in the din
of screaming Puerto Ricans
and
Black People who can only
get drunker and louder
in the twilight of West 78th Street
where
old furniture and new junk
and dead ambitions
melt slowly
Rainy twilight/dreams.

WHISPERING BLASO

Blaso
lives in the middle of Long Island
surrounded by old fashioned houses,
barking dogs and silent men in
sad uniforms who sit and pretend
not to see you as you pass through
their little gate.

Blaso
waits in the big building,
the one with the dead trees
and where the smell of white
tries to hide the smell of urine
and you are asked:
"Are you a relative or a friend?"

Blaso
finally arrives after
a tone poem of banging doors,
clinking keys, muted locks and
feet without shoes, and he looks
asking with a whispering plea,
"Did you bring any ice cream?"

Blaso
smears the ice cream into his mouth
and tells me that he is flying each
night, kissing the stars
but that sometimes the stars

3

hit him in the mouth
and it hurts.

Blaso
tells me that he is being destroyed
by the permissiveness of the blue-eyed
psychiatrist because
chaos is a methodical form of
new therapy / no therapy /
no kissing.

Blaso
drinks new magic elixirs
that transform everything into
restful sleep and stimulated appetite,
relieved anxiety, agitation, hyperactivity
and control all his
undesirable symptoms of magical origin.

Blaso
sings of the great white Buddha
and the masses of white
tell him to shut up:
No singing allowed!
No kissing allowed!
No religious services allowed!

Blaso
is quiet and only moves his lips,
his eyes are closed,
his hands pressed against his chest,
ice cream melted on his face.
"All right mister, he's upset now,
you've got to leave — Visiting is over!"

Blaso
dances away
muttering his song of paradise:
"Buddha, Buddha/my hands/your feet
ice cream and sun flower seeds/
Boy Scout Handbook and Orgone Box/
for everyone."

4

EDWIN ALLEN

CONTRA

Locked in the prison of Objectivity,
The slave of logic,
The forlorn seeker of Illusion,
The starving cormorant,
    Choked by the cord of an unnamed coldness
Is my heart.
Tossed impassively on waves
Of shallow, transient emotion,
Victim of swiftly violent,
Then ebbing, passion.
Unresponsive hearer of words of tenderness,
Spoken from eager, sweet lips
With need, hope and trust.

Lonely inhabitant of temples
And gardens beyond mortal knowing,
Longing to escape,
Wretched, yet loathe to leave.

Becalmed, hanging in space,
Empowered to choose, yet
Unable to choose.

O heart that trusts not itself
And longs to rest
Not in death, but in the
Calm crucifixion of knowing,
Caring, suffering, unafraid.

Heart that cannot die, and
Refuses the gift of life;
Transfixed from knowing and searching
Too much.

Heart that is living, yet unalive,
King that cannot renounce his throne
Nor ascend to it,
Searcher that finds, yet cannot comprehend.

Heart that lives and breathes
The scents of immortal being,
That breathes the fumes of hellish reality
And cannot realize, nor reject.

Beyond sleep, death,
Beyond hope, pain,
In the enigma of a contorted reality
Knowing and aware,
Yet beyond them all
In the clutch of the Nemesis:
Indecision.

O heart, your life is the death
Of the weak and the strong alike.
We know and fear to know;
Arrested at the threshold of
Man meeting God,
We must hope only for release
In Nothingness.

DONALD ANDERSON

CLOSET DRAMA

Pendulum-like, the bobbing of the past
Swings by the eyes, and back again;
A sullen spark, a love-note found
Left in a book, now back again;
A sober flash from out of dead
Mahogany, yet back again;
A musty dewdrop never to
Be suddenly, or back again.

BALLAD OF A MOLE

Homely little Mr. Bluster barely
Caused a stir at all
That day, before the bank, he squarely
Rapped his head against the wall.

Stars and swirls and gangrened thumbs;
Falling bricks and leather slums;
Esses and cees on pillories;
Bubbles, bells and paper crumbs.

Homely little Mr. Bluster lingers
Briefly to explore
The blood he's rubbed between his fingers,
Sighs, and tunnels on once more.

6

TALE OF A NON-BELIEVER:

A Fly between a Window and Storm Window

How in hell you got in there I'll never
Know; but there you are, a fishbowl full of
Frantic-winged frustration, like a eunuch
In a bawdy-house. You'd think you'd bash your
Brains out on the glass, although you must be
Somewhat empty-headed now to keep on
Trying to step through what you can feel
Beneath your feet. And furthermore, while you
Continue butting vainly at that deadened
Mask of light, who knows what evil lurks behind?
Supposing that I opened up the
Sash and calmly plucked off both your wings,
Because I could, you know. And by the way, you
Know damn well that if you get outside
Somehow, when darkness fell you'd only turn
Around and try to get back to the light
Inside, which makes your wings seem just a little
Silly: compared, at least, to dunghill days.

F. MAURICE ATKINSON

A DEATH LOVES

Love,
    Who was a child of man,
Committed suicide one cold autumn night
By   from my bedroom window
   jump
       ing
To the cold, hard pavement below.

Deadly gazed his blood-teared eyes;
Deadly gasped his dying sighs.

But I —
    Could do nothing.

But I —
    Had been loving

      Until this sad

    Disaster.

WATER SOFTENER

Sometimes I get the idea
        That the wide world is beautiful.

I tread water of my mind
Before it cascades and caresses
Some hurts which are enfolded by reality.
I squirm a bit, until I find
That this whirlpool bath is refreshing.
Swimming self to self to superself, totality;
I even drip of thoughts of men,
And still get taste in mouth of freshness
As the droplets trickle to tongue. And equality

       Seems
       A
           Good
               Thing,
If I could practice it. At least

Sometimes I get the idea
        That the wide world is beautiful.

SEEKING

Dying inside,
       As I try to find

That one person
       Who would ease my mind

And carry me
       Far from soullessness,

I search, scrambling
       For a solace nest

Somewhere, and in
       Someone's gracious heart.

Hoping, holding,
       Clutching for a start,

(Symphony which
        Builds on grand refrain)

I reach emptily
        For a love again.

This game, though, seems
        Too tragic to play.

Thus I wander,
        Alone, in dismay.

A. AZEN

BLACK BOY

Bootblack! Yuh burly blackskin boy
Whar are yuh, loafin' dinge?
Yuh git thar on yer shins
And tar them boots o' mine
Yuh hear that, burly black?
Been larn't yer place, yuh buckle
When yer spoke. Black boy ain't fit
To lick the white man's boots!

Man, the. clock's. run. out. on. you.
And. you. don't. even. read. it.
There's something on the wind.
Evers since four score and seven . .
A scent . . . Stronger . . .
Than all the magnolias in Mississippi.

Them shoes yers need no shine
But they do need mendin' bad.
The sole's wore thin, an' the buckle
Bound so taut, it cramps yer gait
An' don't 'low room fer growin'.
Them cowhide shucks
Won't last much mo'
A decade so I 'spect.
So be a man, an' sport yerself
Some honest walkin' shoes.
An' when you buy 'em, buff 'em
Or go barefoot same as me.

I don't wipe the white man's boots no mo'
I ain't no mo' his black boy.

9

LEN BACZEK

WITHOUT REASON
to Rae

To tell you of love, my love,
of the cause and the effect
is beyond my lean logic,
or to sing of love, my love,
and to would the unsung could
is unknown to my meter,
in my illiterate love
I can only proffer that
I loved you before because.

STRANGE ENCOUNTER

When Cleopatra barged in on Antony,
　　Was he caught unaware with his toga down,
Or was the fellow dramatically arrayed,
　　Primed to pose, to make the meaningful gesture,
Or was it time for more florid rhetoric
　　Prepared in the quick panic of the cloaca?
Is it such that jealously eludes annals,
　　A strange encounter disrupting nature's needs?

THE SUNBATHER

In the dog tongued day,
by milk rumped sea and green dance hills
intoned by insect choirs,
in the hair hoisting cold toothed wind,
　　he sings to fish and sandbird
inflamed with a lover's lust.

UNSCIENTIFIC OBSERVATION

Frail virgin of a flower
　　quivering to yourself
　　one day
　　you will fling yourself
　　to the wind
and seduce dancing
　　butterflies.

10

JENNIFER KAY BAILEY

GOLD-TIPPED

There are times in Spring
When I wish I could catch the day
And hold it whole:
One cotton-candy moment, perhaps,
Or a birthday cake frosted in youth
With the sun for the candles
And a blade of grass to cut it.
Or why not a gavotte,
Callioped by a frisky, slightly tipsy wind,
Yesterday but a shivering breeze of the snows.
If I could but snare a day,
Or even a part,
I would store it with care,
Water-proofed and snug-warm,
To flavor lesser days
When the years are colder
And the sun less gold-tipped by Spring songs.

MORNING HAZE

There's a haze on the hills of my heart
And a mist in the valleys below.
The sun has been kind, as too, the rain,
But somehow nothing will grow.

The hills will grow vacant with years
And the vineyards will cease making wine.
But oh for the heart beneath the hills,
Oh for the heart that was mine!

LET US KEEP ALL THINGS . . .

Let us keep all things unto the end.
Let us be wise and not squander our wealth,
But hold the dearest as the last.
Not break with sighs but strongward prove
And make of heartbreaks an alabaster chain
To wear as sign of knowing no regret and never shame.
Thus we must hold our treasured love,
Beholden to a set of images crucified by events long past.
And drink with cups of grapeless wine the health
Of the ghosts, and our hurt, and our love, my dear friend.

11

A COAT OF MANY COLORS

My heart has known lean years,
Has been as Egypt during seven seasons,
But there has been no Nile
            for my heart.
                None.

And parched, it has gone its way,
Through valleys cold with tears
And bitter-hot with sweat,
            and it was
                Weary.

But now, the seven years of harvest
Have arrived, the mirror years departed.
And now the rivers
            (But not the Nile)
                Overflow!

MATTIE BELLE BARBER

CRESCENT MOON

You bewitch me, whisk of a moon
    Gold, lone scimitar in the sky
Witch in emptiness on high
    Dreaming, weaving a rune.

Keeping her distance is a star
    Brightly brave, for all your mystery;
Twinkling hex's on your sorcery;
    An acolyte grinning from afar.

Still, you gleam and cut the blue
    With your double points of light.
Earth-men wrapped at last in night
    Are bewitched, enslaved by you.

REVERIE ON THE SHORE

Roaring and lashing, the waves assault the shore;
    Rugged rocks repel the incessant shocks.
The sand sighs in weary resignation
    Under the inexorable roll and drive
            of the waters . . .

12

Another day . . .
The blue, soft fingers of a gentle sea
  Lave and smooth the yielding stones.
The sands cling lovingly to each wave;
  The sun brings dimples of joy
                    to the waters . . .

Mystery . . .
The waters of the earth, longed-for and hated . . .
                    Good and evil.

BELL AND MIKE

Tell it to Cole, the call-in time on air
Makes calls from all for hours of talk and tell,
Comes through to us who catch the tone and bell
And keeps our thoughts alive to things we share.
We think about some big, well-known affair
Or just reply to one who casts a spell
On those who hear, but not too well,
To get the truth that speaks out on the air.

This lad has got them staying at the switch
Long past the decent hour for sleep
To ring his bell and give a thought they like,
Or as a watch, take time in hand to keep
The guest who calls the friend a witch
From Cole, a fire set to a simple mike.

PAULA BARNES

OUR SONS DIE

Red is the ground in Viet Nam,
Drenched by brave men's blood.
In horror's wailing psalm
They die in heat and mud.
Our dear beloved sons
Gashed by alien guns.
In shot and shell,
In earthly hell,
They gasp out parting breath
In lonely, fearful death.
Is this why we bore them?
Is this why we adore them?
To feed the war god's mill
And other mothers' sons to kill?

13

LET THE LEADERS GO

Let our leaders go
And fight wars of hell and woe.
Let our Top Man and Ho Chi Minh
Pit themselves against death and sin,
In our Armageddon of Viet Nam.
And in the tune of cannon's psalm
There'd soon be no more
Of blood and guts and gore.

SEX

There's a renaissance in sex, they say.
Quite different than in Mother's day.
Now it's loudly proclaimed,
In Mother's day, quietly declaimed.
But, no matter what,
Anti-birth pill, or not,
Brazen immodesty or silent will,
Sex is sex, be it loud or still.

JOHN MARTIN BELL

The smoggy uniforming crud
Is gone
The islands lie a wave from here
Rising as if in protest
From the horizon
In sharpened gashes.
The sea, in revenge
Commands the yielding waves
In all their agony
To pound the helpless sand.

A duck tracks across a tinkling lagoon
Tries a takeoff. He can't
But finds he likes his splashings.

A jet. Throttled well back
Etherializing before my eyes
(Slowly, mind you)
With whatever clouds there are so far away
That they seem like torn up doilies.
And it is simply there
Away
From the laws
Which hand it its legality.

14

And there's a girl
Dancing near the sun
Soaking the salty water
Into her toes
I'm not there
She dances on
In celebration of her loneliness
Proud of her long red hair
And barefoot feet
She'd stop if she saw me
And yet so bravely dances
Before the clapping sea
And me
She is the one
The *only* one.

PATRICIA BENSON

MOTION

Ebb Tide:
Sweeping in
Soothing the shore
    with your refreshing caress
Leaving living jewels
    from your inner depth
    upon a sea shore bound
    by your gems and green sea-grass

Your playmate
    of shifting, sandy shelves
Welcomes your jewels,
And in the dark of winter evenings:
It turns your shells —
    broken, battered,
    by your rough
    innocent play —
Into gleaming eyes,
Watching your inward,
    leaving, forthright motion
It turns them into
    gleaming mirrors —
    sparkling motion.

PAUL V. BEYERL

EXPERIMENT

they were mine.
and he was m'lord
and she was m'lady
living in a glass
kingdom etched with
    greasy fingerprints.
my two subjects
    dressed in their
royal butterfly robes.
and they were in
my power, and i being god
let them live.
and when i tired of
playing god i became
noah
saying
       go ye forth and
          multiply
and they
fell to
the earth
dead.

HARLEQUIN

We have long lived
  in the harlequin
    of the mind.
Where conscience-policemen
    call out
        stand back
  as the perverse
crowd breaks
    through.
  While hell-hot
flesh burns with shame
  at the embarassed
blush
    of thoughts
  and yet
    tramples the
    keep out
       signs . . .

NOBODY KNOWS

sixteen angry feet,
one kicks open the
splintered rail gate
so it flies with spite
onto the lawn. sixteen
angry feet stalking across
the lawn (twenty
square feet of dust
and paper and
rusty tin cans and
rotting apple cores) and
then the porch
quivering with indignation
beneath those feet and
the whole house shaking
with fright of
sixteen (white) feet.

> nobody knows the
> trouble i've seen,
> nobody knows
> but (J) jesus.

old bess on a swayback
rocking chair,
forward and backward
in time to her song.
old bess is happy — her
tom has fled away
safe — her boy is safe.

> nobody knows the
> trouble i've seen,
> nobody knows
> but (J) jesus.

hey coon, hey dirty
black nigger, where are you?
come out and meet your (M)maker.
hey, white man's whore, dirty
black, where's your bastard?

> nobody knows the
> trouble i've seen,
> nobody knows
> but (J) jesus.

old bess sings. angry
men cursing wrath bent

17

on wrecking furniture.
plates, a wedding gift
(Woolworth's, @$.19, but
a gift) but smashed anger
turned frustration.
kerosene lamp dropped,
flames appearing,
old bess singing,
              nobody know the
              (christ get out of here)
              trouble i've seen
              (let her burn)
              nobody knows
              (holy jesus bitch,
                  what a fire!)
              but (J) jesus.

DAYDREAMS

the sun was slipping
through the leaves
like a daydream . . .

i sat there
in the sun.
i sat there thinking
thoughts of love.
i sat there with
happy thoughts of love
and sad,
lonely tears slid
down like the
sun sliding down the
leaves . . .
my arms empty
i sat there
and mused my
love intangible . . .

the sun was slipping
through the leaves
like a daydream
and the leaves were
brown and dead.

TOGETHERNESS

say you love me
and
i'll say i love you
                just
don't ask my name
and
i won't ask yours.

and we'll go
to
bed
strangers.
bonded in loneliness
but we'll say we love,
and
happy the night.

and when the
sun
shines through the
dirty chintz,
please
say nothing,

        wake me
with a kiss,
and silently
            slip
        through yonder
        door,
with just a smile
to
say
good-bye.

NEENA BIRCH

THE IMPOSSIBILITY OF L-O-V-E

There is something, inside,
That gnaws at the syntax of L-O-V-E;
Most often a billowing wonder — uncontainable —
Uncontrollably stuffed into its four letter prison,
Pressing frantically against the wall of "E".

Rearrangement of letters is in vain,
Combinations and permutations cannot erase the harsh
Birth and death of a line.
Perhaps a breakthrough —
An l ^O_e v could grasp the wholeness, but . . .
There is something, still,
Too meager.

There is something incongruous;
An incompatibility hidden in the starched lines
And unmalleable angles of an "L", a "V" or "E",
A misunderstanding between the emotion and the symbol.
The "O" stands singularly alone in any attempt
At aesthetic imagery.
L-O-V-E. The word as such has no use,
When thoughts brim and spill
So alive over the fixed file of letters.

There is something, inside, that moves . . .
A sentimentalist,
A linker of 1000 words of being;
Of feeling, seeing, smelling, hearing
Into a self-made chain;
Weaving three rows of the same into one
Firm and vivid braid,
And joining the beginning and end so that
No seam is unravelled.
And, still . . .
Only a mortal mind's attempt,
Only a sniff at an earth overgrown with flowers.

CARL BJORDAHL

LOVE'S ANSWER

Love is the poet's eternal song,
But love unsung may be as strong.
Does the poet's need
To sing love's deed
Sometimes expiate a wrong?

Conflict begins with Cupid's dart
And the Caliban in each human heart.
Love, silent, pure,
May well endure
Beyond the poet's facile art.

DAN BLOOMFIELD

DRINKING STEAMING TEA

Drinking steaming tea
Needing shave and shivering
From loss of last night's wine,
I breathe apologetically
Like a dishonored samurai;
So as the morning sun
Seizes my dusty porcelain,
I slowly rise to water
Artificial flowers,
And can no longer scent
The pollen wind
In my icy ivory towers.

YOU KNEELING ON LINOLEUM

You kneeling on linoleum
Playing jacks at midnight
And your chubby toe, so pretty,
Just like the golden apple
The goddesses quarreled over.

You expounding Revelations and
Wanting your black curls cut.
Oh Kitchen Aphrodite
In your beat-up white robe
Drinking too much wine
And your inconsolable laughter
Sprinkling sugar on our sour grapes.

I'M SOME SORT OF EVIL GENIUS

I'm some sort of evil genius
jumping through good and evil
as easily as a child
    pees the bed
    or climbs a tree
    or skins his knee
    or makes mud pies
    or cries or lies
    or spins the bottle
    with the pretty kindergarten girl
    next door.

21

IT WAS EARLY AUTUMN

It was early-autumn
in an orchard
and above the trees
only a round, orange, corny, old moon
below it
just you and I
a stone's throw from civilization

It was our first time alone together.
You never spoke a word
just smiled
into the violence of my face
then understanding my man's mind
you   — almost sadly —
undress
bringing your legs into
an open valentine
and suddenly
in the moonlight
your face seems that of a pretty little boy
and I feel like an ancient, Greek queer.

WITHOUT MAP

Without map
      or a penny-bought compass
this kangaroo
      jumps with his diaper down
burning on dreamsteam and unable to stop
      the illogical dancer
      wanting an answer
            in the zoolight
            in the floodlight
but
      f
      a
       l
        l
         i
          n
           g
through the skylight
to splashingly shipwreck
into the bathtub
of dry society.

My God, have I wet the bed again?

22

THE HISSING WHITE STEAM

The hissing white steam
              from the cannery
floats up toward
              the raindrops tonight
while out in the yard
              on pallets
red-wet tomatoes glisten
              under the floodlights
where hiding in the shadows
Manuel
              heats his stomach
              with wine
and is sure
              to catch a cold.

EILEEN BROOKS

OBVERSITY

I always wanted to write blank verse
On the timelessness of time,
But a Ringety-Tingety sounds in my head
And the words dance away into rhyme.

I started a perfectly precious pentameter,
A dactyl, a trochee, and one anapest
But Mother Goose galloped across the page
And . . . I've forgotten the rest!

O, Higglety-Pigglety, here I go
I'm off on a spondee
I'll finish that deathless, breathless ode
When I'm free of this Fiddle-dee-dee.

LOVE

Without aggression there is no love
     says the Behavioral Psychologist
          noting that only ants and men
               wage war on their own kind.

The ant has only his battalions
     but the exquisite weaponry of man
          reaches earth-sickening proportion.

23

I guess that means
    we have more love
        so much . . . that at
    The Last Picnic
        we shall serve
            ourselves up
                . . . Napalm-fried.

ANN BROSSMAN

#1

To be that daisy . . .
        white hands basking in sun

            and nothing else
        except warm breath of familiar fragrance.

And yet, when it rains . . .
        you must be cold, naked flower.

#2

Where is the moment?
Am I tired in a dizzy day?
        Crying, maybe . . .
            wishing,
            talking,
                even . . . Laughing?
Where is the moment?
Is my back turned,
    My head turned?
Why does it mock and slide from my grasp?

I want to capture it in a box and look at it.

JACQUELINE BROXTON

VARIATION ON A NATURAL THEME

As we walk upon this sand that has absorbed the weight of
Countless others. We claim each step to be a dual discovery
In the name of our alliance.

walking while the fog ambles its way
in quietly unnoticed until the whole beach
is covered and we appear as an object.

Treading upon sand, duplicating a pattern, originated before
Eden we move slowly in search of what we accidentally
Found yesterday.

we have journeyed the whole beach now
yet this voyage has given us nothing
to help explain the assumption that initiated
the first step.
there is only the rumble of the sea
to obstruct the noisy silence between us now.

And we pause while the waves complete their cycle
that so much could depend on one moment

What we have discovered we cannot define,
What we have felt we cannot ignore,
A previously extinct need has been disclosed to us.
A need that will not accept the limitations of logic.

that we who have masterminded all
concepts, synthesized all things done everything with the
exception of give a life, should discover.
a hope between two people in a circumstance
of doubt that repels an explanation.

#1

in a whirlwind struggle to overcome my alloted lifetime of,
just one day i pause.
hoping that the things that issued out so much pain on
yesterday will disappear from my circumstance
on tomorrow.
. . . pausing to remember how familiar pain is, and how distantly
strange happiness might be.
so i journey forward to the future turning away
from today confused. for in spite of my partial anticipation
there really isn't anything else for me to search for except
the antique
truth

MARCIA BRUNDAGE

TWO POEMS

Fairy fluff floated
   Striving for the moon
      To soar thy silver stairway —
      Becoming whole

The outstretched claws of the sea
Tearing down all hope
      Plunging into eternal solitude

Jack-O-Diamonds
masters inferiority plague/
    (the mind)

a world awaits
      the golden touch
while chaos
lingers
on her
lips

(avalanche of
      hearts
slipped thru her
      soul)

One's power
vested

    (divine right)

such strength
you reel —

    (falling leaves
    insult)

jack-o-diamonds
  jack-o-diamond
a joker —
    home
    at last

ROBERT S. CAMBURN

TO A LITTERBUG
(with regrets to Shelley)

Woe to thee, blight spirit!
What a bird thou art —
   That on pavement or near it
    Pourest thy discard
      In profuse rain of unappreciated shard.

Higher still and higher
 On the earth thou pilest
  Rubbish by the quire;
   Every view defilest;
    And, traipsing, still dost strew,
    And, strewing, ever rilest.

THE POND

A small boy skips smooth stones across
  a quiet, tempting pond
Where waves the wild grass tall and free,
  and bends the languid frond.
The old mill wheel turns slowly
  like the massive wheel of time,
While sudden ripples, glist'ning, spell
  eternity in liquid rhyme.
Now falls a strange and dream-like hush
  the green and glowing wild-lawn 'round,
And in that moment, brief, bewitched,
  thereon a royal court is found:
A butterfly, in regal dress,
  as though by magic rite appears —
No tyrant he, with haunting fears:
He gaily claims a hundred thrones,
As from the woodland's mystic depths
  ring out his herald's blissful tones,
And courtiers in lesser garb
  their less pretentious places take,
In deference to their sylvan king
  at his secluded lake.
Aflame with morning's golden light,
  the leafy boughs of ancient trees
Watch over one small boy who sees
How swiftly fairy realms are gained
  when Summer waves her gentle wand
Above a tempting, quiet pond.

27

OLD LETTERS

These sacred embers:
I cannot scatter them
To the four winds
And never know them more.

These relics of lost joys,
These windows on sweet days
And hallowed shores long quit
By time's relentless oar,

Too poignant yet for view,
I cannot cover them
With dark oblivion
Forevermore.

ODE TO SPRING

The tulips Persian crowns display,
The daffodils gold trumpets sound,
Bright crocuses scatter rainbows round,
While scillas' royal robes abound,
And frosty snowdrops sway.

To Spring, the Queen of Earth, they bring
Tribute of glad pageantry,
Acclaimed by woodland melody,
Early butterfly and bee,
And every budding thing.

O Paradise, thou art enough,
Dost thou but mimic Spring
With all her radiant flowering,
Songbirds gay upon the wing,
And zephyrs sweet as love.

RAISE NOW THIS NOBLER BANNER

One world, one common world, one world for all:
Design a banner now for this, and be content with nothing less!

O World! The Precious Age impends!
The audacious dream of man awaits the last, the noblest,
        and the bravest deed — of Brotherhood — for full reality.

Raise now this nobler banner o'er mankind:
Heroic, to enwrap the world;
Harmonious, to unite all peoples;
Splendid of color, to exult of the new life;
Exalted with dignity, to proclaim the worth of man.

Rally no more around these ancient flags, these sovereign
      flags of pride and power and useless death:
Raise now this nobler banner and proclaim
One world, one hallowed world, one world for all!

MARY L. CARNES

TRANSITION

Perhaps, 'tis true, Prized Youth. — All things must fade
With time — pale blue of silk, full-blown white rose.
Even the burning pink of sunset glows
At last, into oblivion of night, betrayed
By passing hours. We march in that parade!
The perfume of *being* has scarcely touched one's nose —
A heavenly whiff, when suddenly — life slows
Almost to nothingness. Oh! — Could you not have stayed —
Wild blood that pounds to a "Can't-Wait" meter,
Young heart a-somersault with joy, emotions —
Passion, tender as violets wet with rain?
No, Youth. It is not in spite that a kindly Creator
Slowly weans us from Earth and its foolish notions,
Hearts already transplanted, that long last look bereft of pain!

JAMES CARROLL

OCEAN'S END

From high and empty skies a bird sank down
And slowly circled overhead as if
In hopes that my small boat was long sought ground.
It seemed about to land, but then a whiff
Of man-smell scared it off. The bird back-wound
Its circle then, with quicker beats to lift
Through winds of pain, old weariness and fear.
I heard its desperation screech for rest
And wondered why it flew with no mate near
And why for ocean's end it left its nest.
To share my boat, my second thoughts, my day
I called the bird, but it had flown away.

29

GLENN S. CHAMBERS

The Southwest wind
blowing before high
black rain clouds
sweeps around a corner
of the library
and catchs a cedar
unprepared.
I have seen it since
many times,
bluejays making a ruckus
in the long-needled pine,
raging uproariously
like drunk lords, strutting
the eves outside the library
window.
Now the rain makes
a full warm sound
over the earth.
Will I ever grow tired
of it all?

THE DEVIL DANCE

Shadows incorporeal
vague and slippery
slide stealth-footed
into my aviary
and
all the pretty birds
fondly nesting
are startled
from their eggs,
rainbow wings clattering.

The stealth-footed figures
dancing on my tears
tear my soul
afraid
and so so lonely.

30

GEORGE CHRISTENSEN
SUMMER AT WOODCHUCK

The tall green trees on the mountain side,
A clear brook gurgling from the springs,
The dirt roadway, the log house,
The unpainted shed and
No humanity . . . a rest, a regrouping,
And then again to carry on . . .

ROGER CLARK
LOST

Life started with the sun,
   We're as old as Adam.
We're lost in a world of dalinesque creatures,
   And politicians who act like villains from Chaplin movies.
A world of electrified folklore,
   And surrealistic eye charts.

Death darkens the sun,
   Death finished Adam,
Death will lift us from the delirium of living.

ROBERT C. COATES
TO CASEMENT AND THE REST

*(Commemorating the 50th anniversary of the Irish Uprising of
April, 1916. Sir Roger Casement, Irish diplomat, humanitarian,
scholar & patriot, was executed by the British in August, 1916.)*

To win, to seem to win,
    to lose.
To try, and then, bewildered,
    fail.
Assailed, jaw set, to steel the will
    and fling
(not Brave, much larger than the brave)
    The gauntlet
Flat at the hostile weaknesses, clods, barriers,
    Ride at them skillfully . . .
       Unhorsed,
Perceive more grimly that the soul of man
Is doomed to nowhere man or the hell
Of the most lonely total valor.
He that (alive) contrives to stand the middle ground
    lies, and with the lying,
       dies.

'ALLO, BAYBEE!

'Allo, Baybee!

    I yam mad out from my mind
      in love for you!

This morn, with the moist grass smelling,
    birds alive, (day) alive!
    Me (baby), me Alive.
    Singing, Wild, crazy punching
    frog-leaping, mossback embracing
    Shouting up 23 stories at window cleaners
    Crazy, crazy, wild.

I'm the mad happy-prince,
    commanding my subjects (
      with a punch,
        with a yell,
          with a Ho de Wheee!
            Blast off!
          s
          ee?!

Preciselyright of course. Direct command. get me?.
                              Ho!
Besides, today is Today, yesterday gone,
    all glorious, so Sing!

THANK YOU FOR SORROW

Thank you for sorrow. For:
    Sorrow, the democrat—like death—and leaping joy.
    Sorrow, icon-breaker of poor dullard happiness.
    Sorrow, opener of eyes to men's true lacks, to irony,
      to pain in gusts from womb to earth.
Unnoticed, my joy-cup enshallowed by deposition
    of the sediment of habit,
      of half-remembered times,
        of partial truths,
Suddenly Sorrow!
Deep knife of the upper Nile's flood-time,
    whittle, swirl, grind with pebbles of pain
      incise thy gorge
        thru the debris
          into my soul.
Sorrow, scoup now the reservoir
    which shall in better days empound my deeper joy!
Thank you my dear unstable love, for sorrow.

DAVID M. COLLISON

RICHMOND PARK

Never again such a summer,
   Never again so bright
With the deer in the park at Richmond,
   Shadows against the light.
They scratch an ear with a forefoot,
   Shake, or look up alert
At the boy with the Brownie outfit
Or tripod-and-Canon Bert.

Never again the stillness,
   The people swallowed in space
As they ramble or run at random,
   Or sit at a tall tree's base;
The clarity-sight of drowning,
   The long farewell to it all
Implied by the sharp-etched scenery
   Or the players with brash red ball.

Never again the pleasure
   Sharp as the shock of hooves
Cantering over the pasture
   Toward white-distant roofs.
Tweed-jacket riders in bowlers
   Are one with the ponies' pace
As they gallop familiar grassways
   Past the couples in close embrace.

Never again the laughter
   Empty as people's minds,
The crackling thorny chatter
   And Arcady left behind;
Cherish the pleasant memory
   Of deer lying down to rest
In the long soft shadows of afternoon
   And the sun through the trees to the west.

THE RONDININI PIETA

Forget the statues with their polished limbs,
Grief has no form; why give it time and place?
Give to it sorrow's universal face
For beauty, wisdom destined for the tomb.

33

Forget the legs, too confident and large,
The arm dismembered, from a former view.
What youth could only guess, experience knew
And left it veiled, that charity could charge

All griefs, all wounds, all kindnesses undone
To this one last account, one final debt.
Once paid, the sculptor and mankind forget
And, purged, embrace the Resurrection.

RICHARD CONLIN

THE CANARY

Yesterday I killed the canary
It sang too loud; the world was offended
So I wrung its neck, snuffed it out
Like a moth in a flame, the twin flares
Of my hands despatched it to an end
And I can feel neither glad nor sad; it had to happen
The command came to me from a strident voice
Outside myself; and though it hurt me,
I had to obey; the other day I shot a crow
Though not for the same reason, for the same dictate
And my rifle pierced it without mercy.

THE TROOPS

The troops are laying mines now
The silver-maned leopard is wandering
Over the jewel-topped hills;
The white-haired goat snarls and leaps in its pen
And limping falcons wing across the sun.
Fevers of the atmosphere are calling to each other
Sunspots stagger before our eyes
The flat earth which stretches before us
Is whirling like a dizzy gyroscope —
Lifelike, the dinosaur bones move
Over the shadow of a lonely wharf
And the gremlins of lost counterfeiters
Sail at noon on the tall gray ship.
Creation's mind is whistling, and humans cower beneath its breath —
The air is filled with smog
It takes dark glasses to see things clearly
In the dry moonlight outside.

WESTERLY

The green tragedy of the time —
The wanting of the flame,
The burning thirst for whispers,
And the lights of Caesar's train;
Across the crumbling mountain
That shudders in the rain,
The voice that speaks of starting —
The head that gleams with pain.
Where the forest turns to rainbows
When the gleaning turns to grain
The linen-fastened arrow
Will swerve, and not restrain.

THE MOUNTAIN

In quest of the screaming mountain
The black-winged raven wheels
Over the velvet trees.
The lines of soft dividing colors
Slide to darkness in the veils of the crags
And the yellowing fields call to the rain;
Veering, the raven twists towards the sea —
Lightning flashes between the black clouds
The small fishing vessels crowd to the shore
And the lines of creeping wolves
Snarl in the wreckage of the thunder.

ICARUS

Icarus — taking off, abandoning
The mud of earth, casting caution
To the winds and the leaden gravity
Back to earth; the hungry impotent
Searching for the sky and catching hold
Of but a cloud with the fertile workings
Of his own brain; a herald of the future
Sending trumpet-blasts of defiance
To the fiery gods, and failing;
Alas — poor Dedalus, who knew his limits
And lost a sun; perhaps progress lies in limits
But it is awesome to see
A tall tree, with a burnt top.

35

LAWRENCE CONWAY

BEAUTY: A POINT OF VIEW

Beauty bows before none;
Rather it beckons me,
An acolyte who n'er
Succeeds effortlessly
To keep it in its place.

A thing of beauty has
No faults — yet a thing of
Plainess has no worth. Who
Would be so crass above
To make one think this way?

My soul leaps out to those
Who respect a being
For what he is and not
For what he looks. Seeing
Worth where it is not —
Ah! That's a sin.

CAMDEN COOK

NOURISHED BY THE SEA

Seek not the dark crevices inside
Your soul that have not been said.
They are deep and straight but are
Filled with thoughts of the dead.

Like the pyramids of Kings gone,
The soul is silent in spoken sounds.
But be alone in the dark of it,
And voices start to pound:

"I am the spirit and sorrow you reap.
I am the love that you feel inside.
I am the spirit of you and your God.
I am the life you lived in pride."

"I am the anger you can live so true!
The searing passion of your hate!
I am the one who awakens you from
Dreams of joy, before the hour's late."

36

Yes, voices will pound on and on.
You shake off the dampness of the
Tomb in the warmth of the hot sun,
But the damp is born of the sea.

T. NELSON COOPER

CAPE MAY SEA

Hark!
Do you hear
the sea? Onward . . .
Onward . . . like a drunken
Sluggard, it lurches forth, bends
at the knee, parts its foaming lips, and
Vomits a glob of seaweed on the pebble shore (or
belches forth a bit of green parkbench that still smells
weakly of roseate romance). Quickly, the sheet of
Bubbly foam subsides, striving in vain to
recapture its spume with lacey fingers . . . Hark! The sea steals
back, returns, recir-
culates in the Univer-
sal Flow . . . Moving . . .
Moving . . .
Where . . .?

LOST CHANCE

The August breeze, the pines above
Gossiped softly about our — love?
The moon glowered at me between two clouds
And toppled down its ultimatum:
    "Do not tarry! Love has many calls to make tonight!
    And Cupid will not waste arrows on the
            undecided!"
And yet I could not. What did I know of life to
    understand love?
Now — you and the moon are glowing somewhere else . . .
The raw December wind whips my face in rude rebuke
And the trees curse violently, spitting pine cones at me.
And I? Alone at the park . . .

MORITURI, SALUTAMIS

Alone I sit
And glower at the streetlamp,
Trying to resurrect his every gesture, phrase —
In vain.
Young scholar of Dr. Johnson! Your mind, too,
Was made to grapple with whole libraries.
So soon to bathe your feet in the River Lethe!
Your reflective mind so quickly eclipsed!
Your delicate intellect so untimely aborted by the grizzly
Black hands of gigantic Death!
Silence! You cudgeling Monolith! You
Delight of Procrustes! How you torture me
With your hooked chariot!
      Would that his ephemeral stay
      Had inspired me yet another day.

P.A. COPPOLA

ON FEELING INSIGNIFICANT

I just cannot say
How many snowflakes will fall
On this winter's day —
There in the wood, where winds twist
Sculptures from the frozen mist.

JABBERWOCKY: 1966

O Mugwumps green and Fermies cressed,
    Fear not the pomey Jabberwock;
Nor smower in dark the snipéd
    Jubjub claws, the eyes that talk.

The Jubjub saw through chlorin leaves,
    And Jabberwock from rundy grove —
The cressed Fermies foling reaves,
    And Mugwumps coming, as they rove.

They clome on frow and gulley dark;
    Swung flying sword and mace to gall —
'Til sunlight dwinned and eve did hark
    The end of wex, the end of all.

The stave of voice from Mugwumps green;
    The Jabberwock with pomey tall —
Are never heard but in a dream:
    The one that drolls the end of all.

WINTER BERTH

1

From the East, the cold winter light slowly
    rises — held down by heavy air.
The wind comes, eddying powdered ice into
      patterns on the deck, then scattering them
      over the water like burial ashes.
The buoy bell tolls.
Hawsers and winch-lines dance icen shadows
    on the pilings.
Speckled waters of summer dreams wash the
      hull of the Charlotte B. — a gull
      hovers, echoing its lonely cry.
Through thinning haze the lighthouse moves
      toward the wharf, inviting moored boats
      to sea.

2

Raoul is Michelangelo, chipping ice from the
      rigging
With measured strokes.
The shower of fragments from his pick makes
    a rainbow — the larger pieces splash.
A fish comes up to see — a gull goes down to eat.
The rigging clear, two seagulls sit, sounding
    annoyance at men.
Raoul chips at winches; others at lifeboats,
    gunnels, gears.
A staccato symphony, off-key when a pick
    strikes metal.
A cloud moves over the boat and
    heads West.
An invisible hand moves the hanging gull.

ANNE CORBIN

WHO ARE YOU

Who are you —
Spitting hatred
From
Your lips
Creating ugliness
Where
Beauty was?

39

Where are you —
In paradise,
Or
In a hell
Of
Your creation?

What are you —
With a venom
That
Fouls the air
And makes
Men bleed
Within?

MY SON

Where is my son
    That I have waited for so long?
Where is his laughing face
    And freckled nose?
The muddy footprints
    On my kitchen floor,
The shedding dog that follows
    Him into the house?
Where is the love that floods the house
    Like summer sunlight?

I've waited for so long.
    Where is my son?

UKRAINE FARMER

He walks the rain soaked steppe alone.
The essence of his dream
Has been destroyed.
He watches jealously
The damp, black earth,
His patch of turf,
As others plow his soil.

No longer can he let
The ground fall
Through his hands
Exulting in its
Ownership.

The work brigade
Walks the furrows
Of his field.
Their sweat falls
On the upturned soil.

The apple trees no longer
Bloom for him alone.
They bloom
Collectively.

E. H. COWLES

A SWEET SMELL OF DEATH

sugar-cured ham
and pecan pie
delivered
    with a tearful
eye
    received by the
children with
    halloween
glee
    and i
a visionary
    at best
consider why
    it was death
that made my
    neighbors
neighborly

RECESS

a blur
red and yellow
    with
    sticks
waist high in
    cool
    grass
hunting lions
    and
little girls

41

```
            engrossed
    in
            tea cups
    on a table top
            rock
    in the cool
            grass
    hunters
            crouch
    for the kill
```

MARCH

```
all the warmth
and
    restlessness
        of youth
charged up hill
from
        the equinox
        binding the branches
of the maple
        still stiff with
winter
        and
            catching
        the wind
in sails of summer dreams
        rounded
the orchard
        fence
where reluctant frost
        clings
and
        the first truth
resides in green
```

NIGHT RAIN

```
a slow awareness
        of soft
                sounds
the breathing
                of
                    the wind
a sweaty hand
```

```
                descends
             to caress
      the slumbering
                   earth
  where seasons
             of seeds
         are planted
                and reaped
```

TWO POEMS

```
in death's dark
          veil
i feel no ill
beside myself with
          optimism
today is not
          armageddon
and it isn't even
          raining
```

```
                carolina
                may be
                finer
      in the morning
                but
      death is better
                in
      the evening
                after
      the lamp is
                lit
      against darkness
```

PAUL CUMMINS

THE DOMESTIC

Disheveled clothes and frazzled hair,
Blear-eyed, mush tongued and thoroughly drunk,
The old woman staggers to her purchased room
Surrounded by junk in the televised gloom.

43

BETSY DAVIS

BIRTH OF A REVOLUTIONARY

In this day of push-button can-openers
I stood
    waiting
Before a door
    waiting
It wouldn't open.
Three years later
I died still
    waiting
And on my tomb it said:
    She stood
Waiting
    Before an old-fashioned door
Waiting
    For it to open modernly
and died
Waiting.
Don't you *see:*
    Push a little
    While you can.

III

    oh Freedom!
    an opulent serpent
    reposing on a sidewalk
      squashed flat.

VI

    past my car window
    meandered trees and lovers
    attached to the grass.

IX

    the winter sky
    sat upon darkened hills
    precipitating dandruff.

POEM

the moon grins lopsided
at those who know love.
definitely indefinite
it is chased by a cloud.
a star winks its eye
at the lonely blank sky.
should the moon's path
    rushing
meet that of the cloud,
the cloud is first alight
then the moon's face
    is blacked out
in the question of space
and the period of time.

ODE TO THE IBM

i am an individual
   number
no two numbers are
   ever the same!
i am individual
   310691.
at least i am odd
though punched full of holes
and clipped at the corners
   like everyone else.
i am snug and secure
    in
my file-cabinet-place
   i move through life
with mathematical precision
my aim in life is
to achieve zero.
that's hard — you have to subtract —
but with the help of my
   mother and friend
the old IBM
   i can do anything
to abstraction.

WINTER STYLE

saw a pair of fur-lined boots
        suspended
from a pair of knees
        and snugly settled upon all that
i also viewed a hat
        that
was wearing knees and boots
too cold to be coherent.

GERALD F. DAVIS

A QUESTION

Ask!
    Was I told?
Ask!
    I did!

    Of what season?

    Snow
    So white and cold
    wind
    so bleak and sharp

    Despair?

For snow
So white and playful
For wind
So free and useful

Winter!

    Of what I seek
No answer is twice.

PRIVATE BEAUTY

A Tree!   I See!

But Wait,   one, two
oh three, but again many times more.

It is the place!   the very place.

I know it well, a simple cool and shaded place.

The woodsman's axe has never known,
nor has the farmer's plow or hunter's foot.

The gentle deer knows it well and passes often,
as the fluffy bunny and fuzzy squirrel do.

I often go there just at sleep time.

But always alone.

To hear the small and friendly birds,
sing as soft and clear.

A wondrous place it is, with but one regret,
it can live only as long as I.

JACK DONAHUE

OUT OF SEASON

A few floating leaves
Demanded my touch
My glowing wisdom crushed their flight
Casting all shallow remains
Toward the flat surfaces
Of irrevocable charm

Some rise again
Piercing not my inner layer of sinful patience
But the outer extremities of justified imprudence

I then prepare a flight for myself
And leave light tracks
Little time passes
Before the acceleration of misled guidance
Turns them brown

Now wilted, presently unaware
Of my destination
They crave for the consolation
Of each other's misery

No matter what season
I can find still a leaf
Harbouring on its thoughts
Of relentless and gay spirit

Waiting its turn for me
To sniff the fragrance
Of bright and shiny magic

Blowing in the wind's
Green and untouched delight
I forsee the cradling of you
In strong hands
And ever-so-gentle mind.

ACCORDING TO THE SCRIPTURES

Lonely hearts share secrets
With friendless boys
Across the seas

Beautiful minds and ugly bodies
Stay home together
Sipping bitter doses two by two

Single-filed compatriots doomed
Can only see hairy necks

Obese children buy trophies
And lie later on

Haggard has-beens have not
Of what not

Yesterday's papers are bought
By dying men and women

Where lost weekends prevail
Miserable weeks lie ahead

Fathers of good boys everywhere
Sleep far away in alleys
Where refuse cans serve as kitchens

One day disgusted
I took the chance
And strolled through the Gates of Hell
There, on a high hill,
Painting in his blank book,
A minor prophet inquired,
"Did I leave anything out?"

ELLEN DOTY

TWO POEMS

My world now: Green crystal, softening plum and burgundy
zebras sleeping in the green circle sungrass. Yesterday there
was nothing, today this — need I move?

They tell me it doesn't exist. Then I am as unreal. We
are one. Can't I show them? They may never know we exist unless
I show them. But their eyes are closed, and they won't even cry!

I cry, and my zebras lift their heads to the grooving
shaftless wind. They smell the sage, become wise, and return to
the wind a dream they've individually shared. Wait.

There should be no tears. I'll join you. We'll only leave
the fences down, then, forever.

Sublimity met tranquility on a winter's day. They waved
hello and wrestled in the snow. They stood of cold and ran to heat
on one some winter's day.
Fortune arrived on a sparrow, steed which landed gently at
their feet. They blew of know and buried it softly in the snow.
They mounded grave flake by flake, sublimity one, tranquility the
other, flake by flake they mounted grave, and pine-scent blanketed.
They mounded grave and sang to save, of rare and sweet to sparrow
steed so softly buried at their feet, and pine-scent pillowed. They
sang to save and mounded grave by flake by flake by flake by flake,
and white tulip seeds were softly thrown by sadness hands. "O
mourn," they sang, "but not for long — old fortune, listen to our
song! For we have met and well we know, and well we triumph in
the snow."
Sublimity met tranquility on an April day. They waved
goodbye and wrestled with to cry. They rose to speak and silent
sat on one some April day. And they sang to mourn of fortune's
steed who, buried softly by their feet, gaily flew away.

DALE DOYLE

AT AVONBROOK

On the mountain the breaker,
Blatantly beating,
Rumble-grind thunder,
Repeating,
Thrumming a vapid, vaporous mist-day,
A waterflail-waterfall watermarking
Watery wassail!

Washerman or washerwoman,
Timpano counterpoint ever,
Never a crescendo on earth's surface
At least!

Depth-deep sequins in the seraglio,
A searing day-serenade,
The consequence of carboniferous
Upper, lower, all-about, *pointe!*

No polemics about poltergeist,
No deathrattle at the deathwatch,
But a deathsman
With a death's-head
Steadily mumble-shrieking it!

MINE DISASTER

Acerbity of apprehensive wait,
Selling strivings and singing hopes,
Accumulating intense high-tension
For fence-fended, repugnant faineance;
Life-waits, death-waits, much-many waits
Circulating about engrossed faces
Straining to see, so too, straining to know
(As a Davy-lamp penetrates darkness
Below; darkness which solidly grips
A man's shoulders and strives to shut his way).

Ingroaning trembling of conquering death
As rare it is that all will escape doom;
Some relieved in joy from deadening stupor,
Some bitter-distressed, their despair complete:
What emphatically is already thought
First ingrowingly sweeping the senses
After the first implacable, shrieking alarum
Screams its doleful, trenchant soul-scraping woe.
Anguish indigenous to coal areas.

A.H. DRUMMOND

TWO POEMS

My hand moves
slowly
across the table
over the
slick
oil cloth
and
stops.

My breath cools my arm.

A child
cries
across the court.

I slip quietly
through
the day
making only
the slightest
ripple.

Too deep to touch bottom,
too cold getting out,
I sink to my mouth
and, floating,
hang there.

My bones slip
out of my
flesh
and clank
together
to that
old tune
I've been
humming
for years.

51

It goes:
"Here we go
round the
mulberry bush,
the mulberry . . . "

I sang that
when
I was
five
around a
wind-blown,
stunted
tree behind
Hailey's house
(hill-crested)
on a late
summer

day
holding hands.

Slowly my
flesh (which
has other ideas)
melts away,
but the bones
slide back
into place.

Again
my clinging
skin
hangs on
its rack
complete —
bones, flesh,
me — preserving
the form.

NANCY ELKIN

THREE BREVITIES

What a phenomenal lot we risk on chance,
on the cold immobile swing of opportunities
which speaks of not going blind before the kiss.
If i were to bet all now   on the counter-run of probability,
perhaps i could see you again,

> When you first came,
> did they tell you what you had got yourself in for?
> There's so much they leave out:
> the goings and the comings,
> the sudden drop of luck into a
> garden of perfume and fresh leaves.
> And as they say in the northland winter-time,
> how are you finding it?

This weekend there may be a letter or a song
grabbed up from dresser to hand,
the most potent reminder of things past.
I have never before chosen to argue
with forces beyond my control,
but couldn't they have picked a mail strike
more convenient to the waiting?

SPEAKING OF INFLUENCES

To be up early
and out in the mist
is to hear Stacy's voice of
a year and four years ago
talking of how it is.
What a golden-haired boy
to be saying the words for us,
and the few of us who remain from that time
jumping up and exclaiming,
Yes — we recognize this also!
Still, we threw him in the lake,
the bloody martyr, only to have him
return the cool hero and jazz us all.
Which probably goes to show
that articulation isn't everything.

CELEBRATION

How to put this thing to you,
a love poem of both the intimacy and the import,
twice-told a tale in the wanton country of your hair,
forests of maple and pine and clean-scented branches.
    Not ever having to ask for more than is given
    when all is given, unasked for
    because, as you have said, you live for other people
    and know what they would ask before they ask it.
      "Fear is not the answer for the few"
      who hum, chew gum, and taste of mist and dew;
      i am not afraid these fine days coming
      and in the "coming" am affirmed and purposed.
Offer comfort up for comfort
above the fortress of your feelings;
not to bridge the moat but fly beyond it
(my mouth brushing yours, your eyes of sun-warmed ground).
    Half-hearted not, the fabled, gifted mold —
    not to be met in hintertime of then
    but now and soon and maybe even later:
    we share these things again though snowflakes melt.
And what smooth fire of cheek and throat
and forehead have i found in inner times?
Just this: that when the arrow speeds and
right before it hits our heart is struck
    by sudden knowledge gained alone away
    which grows with things discovered all anew —
    these intimations of the world's green pastures here
    to graze, survey with wonder, and be grateful.

GOLDBERG THE ENGLISH PROFESSOR

has burned up six hard-fired
months of my life,
and i am here, slowly recovering
from his first-degree flame.
            "What to do when the imagination fails?
            How do we stop to judge the validity of
            experience? What is the nature of the
            adult problem?"
So partly in jest and partly in test
we came to be hooked into strong-arming
a friend past her eighteenth birthday
and out of the rut called aloneness.
Unfortunately without much success.
Because the first thing they often teach you
when you cross over the line is that,
as he has called it,
the only unforgivable misaction is
an inordinate concern for endings.

TOLERANCE DEFINED IN TERMS

of what we do and do not put up with
is not nearly so accurate as
whatever we discover ourselves
to be avoiding with distaste.
You are right to say how
horribly unfair it is for them to
brand Ellen into a defensive and mocking mold;
but although you suffered,
you could never have been
— it defies conception! — anything
less than endlessly pleasant
to look at or to be with as company
on sunny afternoons.
You may be slight, but you are not slighted,
(if you will abide an amateur's pun).
So i tend to think that not being
coarse-grained like the rest of us
makes it that much nicer
when you settle down to our troubles
with a low-slung gravity instead of scorn.

THE NAME OF THE GAME

Does it amuse you to discover
that although you are happy here,
your contentment is so easily undermined,
so easily subverted?
Take the time, dear girl, to
sit back and recover your losses;
there'll be plenty of chances later on
to remake the mistakes you
never seem to learn from.
If you were to read slowly through the repertoire,
you would know that such things
can be made up for,
regardless of how pessimistically viewed you are,
or how low-down, unscrupulous, underhanded,
or violently dirty-minded your vision may seem.
We are often pushed ahead against our will.

VICTOR M. ELLISON

Be aware of
fangs striking flesh —
blood . . .

Death bees stinging —
Honey . . .

Buzzards clawing carrion —
Decay . . .

Overall —
       A burning sun thirsting —
       Drinking blood, honey —
And in the end devouring
       The striking of flesh
               and
       The clawing of decay.

PLAYGROUND

In the playground children shouting —
cries of youth and joy.
And in the void forlornness of a mind
that sits watching their cries
echo, echo — repeating forever —
The mind reliving its own young cries
never returning — yearning —
yearning for its own lost youth —
sinks into the depths of sorrow,
fades into forgetful sleep . . .

While the playground cries grow louder
another world within the mind
hopefully drowns the echo of their cry.
A world of blue skies —
with children of its own —
The mind shouts and skips and sings
playing a long lost part in childhood games.

JOYCE EPSTEIN

THE SEARCH

I am shadow on the wall;
Home of nestling vines.
Trace their weaving climb;
Yearn to reach, embrace, rise.

I am shadow along the path;
Moving on life not feeling, not being.
Should sun take a shine to me,
Swallowed, shadow bows to Being.

HOW MUCH?

You say that I love "too much".
But, who is to say what is too much?
The bird and the redwood stretch for the sky.
Then tell me, why shouldn't I?

I will never say "too much" for love,
But it could be "too little."
And when it no longer is too little,
We can rejoice that it is also not too much.

56

THE INNER "EYE"

It is not as you say,
What I feel from within.
But how can I spell
What words cannot tell?

And if you fail to "see"
What is felt but cannot be said,
Then to continue unseen
Is an end to understanding; death.

But I want you to understand;
To be near as I ascend.
Sharing with you the joys,
As once we shared pain.

MICHAEL FIDLER

SATYR

Women surround me, faces flashing,
Pretty, sexy, multiple pleasures.
From them all tongues are lashing.
From smile to smile, what treasures.
I love you, and you and also you.
So much emotion overtaking me,
I can't move, what should I do?
A thought of running, of being free.
A river coursing through my mind,
Sweeping all toward their destiny.
I can't control this burden, this grind.
End pretty faces and voices that appall.
Up, run, run never stopping,
Leap, lunge, crawl, go away from it all.
In my ears a sick sound popping:
I must go back where gay voices call.

DAVID FILER

MOVING OUT

I was moving out.
I had paid the final
rent, and worked
all day cleaning:

watching a young girl
lying beside the pool
     my pictures were off the wall
     and wrapped and what furniture
     I had I had given away —
     only a soft chair and a small
watching a gull's
white belly against
the evening fog
     table. I swept and mopped
     the floors, scrubbed the oven
watching moonlight
through a curtainless window
     with some lye-base solution,
     cleaned the sinks and the
     table and shined the chrome
watching a lightswitch
alone on a bare wall
     fixtures, kitchen and bathroom,
     then went to bed and lay
awake with my own sounds
in an empty wall.

JAMES K. FOSTER

THE BIRD

Circles, soars, dives, dies
Dying as he dives.
The circle is meaningless treasured beginning.
Soaring is sore — futile gesture
Declining greatness.
Dives best.

Small hearts memory
Cries for
Things past undone.
Aspiring dreams, not of future,
Old age comes young and death can be bloodless.

BECAUSE

The knowledge I am going to die
Makes life the shorter.
How long will you refresh

The last chance,
The planned life?
What good to worry?
The indefeatable armies of unconquering souls
Pervade the lie.
They lay irresolute.
Just another free ride.

WILLIAM HARRIS FREEMEL

CULMINATION OF EXISTENCE

Retribution in the sunlight —
Escape from the bleak red.
Dauntless against the sea —
Cowardly versus reality.

Pretentious is the secure air,
Freedom lingers elsewhere.

Exorbitantly the masses march on —
Then off . . .

Between the blues uneasiness exists.
Capricious, the winds shift —
And the march begins.

Failure leads to jealousy.
Lack of apathy reciprocates evil.

Freedom lies at trail's end —
Settle for less . . . ?

BRING ON THE NEW

Like serenity at the end of a storm,
Or sanctuary from emotion —
It's gone with the setting sun.

Coming and going with few regrets,
Following the fleeing wind —
Secure with the dauntless glow — from a fear within.

Eternal freedom in the realm of death?
Emptiness waits without.

The ends justify equality —
The means justify purpose —
Apathy and greed are nonexistent — infinity rules supreme;
An old generation goes out — equality and uncertainty enter.

LONELINESS

Emotion touches all.

Stars design the mold.
The falacy of boldness depicts the lost.
Outline casts but a glow;
Sullen voices enhance a portion — amiable tenderness.

Self asteem — nature — love
Forsaken?

The lonely are the stars.

Flash of lightning . . .
Warmth and tenderness appear.
Loneliness dissolves — completeness.
Stars shine, they illuminate the soul.

Fancy controls a weak heart —
The mind rests unsure.

Love is gone . . . Or was it . . . ?

The perennial search continues,
Is it to be found? By me . . .

LINDA FULLER

THE BEGGAR CHILD

A gap of centuries has left us strangers.
Yet you remind me of others I know,
Except the crevices of their bodies are
        not filling with decay.

And the cankers have reached your mind.

You are not akin to me.
I cannot understand your voice.
It is small, it is unsure, yet its
        boldness disgusts me.

I do not feel that we are brothers,
For I cannot be human when you approach.
Sand flows in my veins, they
        tighten, they ache, they grind.
Very soon it reaches my eyes, and
        I am blind.

But you know I'm there, you can't
        care if I'm still human.
I don't like you.

I can turn from you but find I
    am facing nothing
        except myself over again
And we are of sand.

60

ROBERT DAN FYFE

TO A SNOWFLAKE

Hasten, Snowflake, join your mates.
Flutter down to find your berth
Among the deep'ning horde on earth.
Though dim's your fate, don't hesitate —
You are nature's modest gift.
For unlike rain you make no sound
To boast your heav'nly fall to ground —
You don't drop; you merely drift.
Your lovely fashions will amaze
A soul apart from mundane ways.
From your elegant carpet of white
Man should receive abundant delight.
How could your wondrous act of grace
Become a gift that men deface?

NANCY JEAN GALL

SO EMPTY

Smiling simply in my sleep . . .
    Looking through the greenness . . .
    Talking to the wind
    And trembling at the sound of bees.
Holding onto nothing . . .
Stepping into an emptiness . . .
Running madly in the night . . .
    Touching stars with my fingertips
    And reaching up to clouds and angels.
Interlocking my mind with No one's
And worshipping the dew in the grass.

Hearing imaginary boats on the churny river
    Drinking only to No one's eyes . . .
    Grasping to a vacuum . . .
    And hugging the non-world.

Working frantically, sweating, exerting
    Only
        to shower into
        cleanness
            and
        emptiness
           again.
So empty, so nothing!

RIDDLES

Incredible inconsistencies climb over
One another as if young brothers
At play in a grassy backyard.

Indescribable longings and more
Knowing truths are on opposite sides
And only the end of the game
Shall reveal "x".

Inseparable am I with what
Shouldnotbe.
My report card is a riddle of mixed-up
Worldlinesses.

TIME, THE DATE-MAKER

Is liberalism a fad?
Time knows and doesn't care.
I don't know and do.
Roses are red, violets are blue,
Nothing matters,
And people kidnap babies and
See flying saucers.
We moved into a house
That can be measured with a ruler.
God is dead and Christ is alive;
Today is E-a-s-t-e-r.
I'd rather be barefoot in Madrid,
I'd rather spank my children,
I'd rather kiss Negro pigtailed pseudo-angels.
I'm in love but no one cay say what the hell that means.
To have a conscience implies possession of inherent goodness.
Who can tell if we wasted time or spent it
Beautifully?
My love say "Be careful."
I say "What of?"
Life is life and death is death,
Hell is earth and heaven is no place.
My grandmother will be buried a hundred times.
Alarm clocks are cruel bosses, and Mondays chuckle among
Themselves and wonder why people listen.
My grandmother will die a thousand times,
Poor, wise, old grandmother.

I WANT . . .

To build towers to the moon
And chase stars in my bare feet —
And laugh, head-thrown-back at the blue-blackness.

I want fingerpaint that's
Green — bright green — and yellow
And brown —
I want to s-m-e-a-r it all over
And make a new milky way.

I want strings — millions of strings —
And I'm going to tangle them
Into knots — that will never come apart
And I want to scatter them — everywhere.

There must be clay — to walk in and
Feel and shape and hold and
It must be gray and perfect.

I want to stretchandstretch —
And grow taller and taller
And see more and more
And say Things to people.

I want to dance and play and
Whisper stories about elves
And toss daisies in the streets.

LISA GALLUCCIO

SUBJECTION

Such a fragrant, fleeting thing
        is the essence of one's self,
Struggling for communication
        through the ever-present pelf.

Boxed in by our earth-bound shadows,
        the substance of one's self,
Swings, suspended from the gallows;

Battered, bludgeoned, victimized,
        by materialistic stealth.

63

STEPHANIE GETZ

DIALOGUE IN E FLAT MAJOR

"Which way doth the wind go?"
he whispered to me
and I to my friend answered
"It goes in a direction which rustles the leaves."

He turned again to me and asked
"Can we rustle the leaves as the wind does?"
I mumbled my answer
"No, we can not move the leaves unless we know
why the wind blows."

AN INDECISIVE AGE

He smokes a cigarette in the closet while his parents are out
to dinner. He argues with
his mother and then goes to his room to cry and pout.
He reads his favorite myth
seven times
and watches boys sailing their toy boats on the pond.
He listens to the chimes,
then cleans his drawers and finds his old magic wand.

MICHAEL D. GIBSON

THE EPITOME OF LOVE

The epitome of love . . .
Yes, love epitomizes itself.
We breathe. That is enough for love.
He who catches the heavens winking
Like soft dew on a nocturnal green
Catches also the whispers of
A dying wind which fetches forth
Only a few morning prayers.
The rest come by themselves;
For as the sun rises,
We glimpse a morning-glory
Kiss the gentle air with its
Blossom. Lo, the quiet day,
And prayers reach the soft hand
Of a child, the frisky feet of a colt,
The silver head of a fountain.
Everything living is touched by
Prayer — by love. It whispers softly,
Whispers and moves on.

MY LAGGING AMUSEMENT

My lagging amusement
Somehow touches me.
I wonder at the pale fires
Which light my brain;
For I'm conscious of the
Softness in my world —
How the weak bulbs above
Relieve the weary streets
Of its filthy scene.
I know that trash collects
Along its quiet gutters.

See how the dullness
Of the sky never reflects
More than a mere
Shadow after dark.
I watch the moon,
Tired of other watchers,
Sneak carefully away
Down thirteenth street.
But it can't escape that
Humorous chase by clouds.

Those puffy masses
Serve me well.
I can rely on them to
Erase my beguiled moment.
I see a pale light elsewhere
Which beckons me to
Suffer, with a yawn,
Thoughts of my
Passing evening, and
I push myself
Slowly home to bed.

A BIT OF WISDOM

A bit of wisdom
Here and there
Is all that keeps
Man from despair.

A mortgaged car
Plus wear and tear;
Taxes, ulcers,
Loss of hair;

65

And bills that I
Would damn unfair
Have made a loan shark
My sole heir.

A bit of wisdom
Here and there
Seems lost in nature
Lost somewhere.
But if you're lucky,
Something rare,
A hairy hand will offer you a banana.

CHARLOTTE GILLETT

NOCTURNE

The night is dark;
The moon rides high;
I sit enthroned upon the hill;
I wait, expecting God to speak,
But all is   still.

LEE A. GLADWIN

DEHYDRATED MAN

Self arose in aureate mist
    from an amethystine sea
And shone at the threshold of aurora:

    Watched where dream, once,
with shimmering steps,
    Walked upon lambent waves
toward being;
    Saw identities
reduced to integers,
    Where men, afraid
of their own aliveness,
    Sought security
in society's vegetable patch.

    Self arose midst effulgent stars
        from the night of non-entity
And died on the altar of expedience.

66

MARGE GLUCK

DESTRUCTION

The shadowed world
Of tall repose
And miles so bleakly laid
The harsh resound
Of the brittle creeks
And fields so crudly plowed,
The deepening wave
With white foaming crest
So bluntly punctured now
The obstacles tossed
And weather beaten tracks
All strewn in place of life
The obsolete man
The insolent man
The power hungry oblique man.

JUDITH B. GOODENOUGH

FAIRY TALE

Pale as a lady, autumn is
The captive servant of the year,
Too fair, too gentle to be his
To work his ugly labors here.

Pity the lady and her skill
Subservient to such a law,
Constrained to sit upon the hill
And spin gold backward into straw.

NORMAN ROBERT GORDON

SAND

Sand — only sand through my fingers.
And the swell of salt waves thrashing foam
On the sand — only sand.

And I sift.
Only pebbles — pebbles in sand.
But I sift — only sand.

67

And a gull swoops to rest
On the sand, pecking at sand,
Finding just sand.

A rotted wood cross stands
In the sand; bones under sand.
Sand, and no soul — only sand.

One last tear in the sand,
Lost in the sand and unwept.
Now sand in my face, in the wind — only sand.

PHILLIP GORDON

LAMENT

Life is —
Hours long,
Minutes short,
Years late.
Mistakes made,
Chances regretted,
Accidents,
Mixed together
And spiced with
Uncertainty,
The sweet taste of
Things all too soon
Gone.
Howl at the moon,
Scream at the wind,
Cry foul to the stars.
But there is no answer.

SUNDAY

Heads bowed, voices buzzing,
Amen, amen, Amen, amen
"Let us pray" (cheaper by the dozen).
Amen, amen, Amen, amen
God is with us, we are God.
Amen, amen, Amen, amen
Pass the plate, we reap what you sowed.
Amen, amen, Amen, amen

WILLIAM C. HADDAN

DRAGONS AND PEACOCKS

So does Youth
    ride Dragons and Peacocks,
    made of papier-mache.

What then when rains come
    and you may watch
    colored papers melting away?

What then for your pleasures
    so full, so rife?

Ride bulls and sows
    to the markets of life.

ONE WARM YEAR

How many seasons? Four?
How many my years? Twenty-two? Twenty-four?
Superfluous seasons, inadequate years.
There was only one year that was warm.
Winter cold shakes and raises skin;
So much better the warmth of fires.
But my season never changed;
Perpetual coldness in need of an inner fire.
She came and gave that one warm year.
Then years of lost summers joined hands
And like mirror-men, reflecting her,
Danced and spread yellow everywhere.
Ridiculous happy yellow, coloring everything, blinding!
Anything not touched, a dull grey beside it.
Hearts expanded with heat
Till they fused, broke, and melted with happiness.
Then in the midst of summer she left.
How sad, that life goes on;
Should the world not stop and mourn?
It does not; no one ever notices.
Now I wait for warmth to come.
An hour of it, a day, a month will do.
But she's gone and will not return,
And candles cannot be suns.

69

JEFFREY CHARLES HARDY

THE HIDDEN RHYME
"Heard melodies are sweet, but those unheard . . . "
John Keats, *Ode on a Grecian Urn*

The hidden rhyme,
How its gnashing teeth prevail far beyond the din of hail
On the steeple's chime.

Listen to its unknown glory,
Silent, rocking oratory,
Making fools of greater poets
Who retell their wonted story,

While forgetting over time
The hidden rhyme,   .
How the postulating pulses make rhetorical convulses
In the mind!

Hear the throbbing of the chasms'
Weary decadent decline,
Watch the dewdrops' simple prism's
Eye make out the secret line,
And the impulse of a heartbeat
Balanced on a slender tine,
Thus making simple certainties

So often hard defined:
The hidden rhyme,
How the melancholy heart becomes the fruit of such an art's
Secret pantomime.

Listen to its soft iambics
On the pavement of the world,
Watch the feet glide o'er the lovesick
As their hearts become unfurled,
Feel the gaieties of freedom
With the verse of the Divine,
Sing the hymns of fallen heroes,

Who, forgetting over time
The hidden rhyme,
How the catacombs of death echo dark and haunting breath
In a verse sublime!

70

Feel the creeping sense of pathos
As you write with pen in hand,
While your thoughts ebb out beneath you
And your mind has lost command.
The secret truths will start to chill
The soldier in your spine,
Then getting to the substance of
What makes great men Divine:
      The Hidden Rhyme!

ALDEN W. HART

TWO POEMS

The old gray master once might tell
of minor evil and dark spell.
A cast of wonder on the soul
A giant effort with no goal.
The present temper can't condone
An elfen goddess on a throne.
A shell of murky mist is now awry
The might mortal mass drowns out a cry.
The small voice speaks now in shadow's tone
The tiny spark of soul, a catacomb.
The image now is burned to golden haze,
A quiet settled mist, solution to the maze.

A hollow awesome pit before me lies,
Its gaping jaws an invitation cries.
An empty soul to soul rings true in hate,
A sparkless soul to gather, now by fate.

On time's eternal plane, infinite cross,
The changeless from the changing to engloss.
The critic point of ne'er desired return,
An essence born in form of breeze to learn.

NICK HEAD

BOAST OF THE GOD

I am Life,
　　one unto myself.
Kill me,
　　and you kill yourself.
Hurt me,
　　and you hurt yourself.
Love me,
　　and you love yourself.
If you love me,
　　you will love my brother.
But only by loving me long and hard,
　　will you learn to love my brother, . . . Death.
Seek out the many facets of my character,
　　and you will wander in the depths of your soul.
Appreciate me,
　　and you will live Life,
　　　　And that is the ultimate.
But ignore me,
　　and you will search forever,
　　　　for something you will never find.
For I am Life,
　　one unto myself.

JAMES HERSH

TRIPTYCH

I

The death of evening
begins to smell
as the blood cakes

the soldiers pass
wondering of agony
and the afternoon's cry

the bodies peter
the limbs long gone limp
tell of an absence.

72

II

Such torture is unknown
save for the great stones
weighing down upon the mind
polished into twin horns
— the remaining, ineffable.

III

I took my own
across the mountain
where they saw
with their own eyes
a vision
unclouded by the hunger
of the empty deserts
of memory.

NO MORE

no more

death has become a bore
        and my mind grown lean
            reaching

no more

I lay aside accoutrement,
        topple the rusted arch
            decorated a thousand times

            I stretch my limbs
            and howl

(the fix
    the traffic of exploration
            of the streets
            that reach

            to ignite my eyeballs

the ground of mystery
            lies smoldering
            in the dormant skull)

no more
    are the stars to breed ethics
            and vagrant religions
            (prophets of hungry solutions)

what remains
                    is the echo chamber,
                    the spiraling fall,
                                        the shriek
and the sharks.

terra firma
was my father
                              my grandfather
                              was a clown
                    my mother's arms
                    now droop
the ancient pottery dissolves
the clay head is crumbs
I sculpt two nostrils and a navel
                              out of air

I am the skipper of an aging hulk
        wandering through the myriad of small rooms
        nauseous
                as it lies in the harbor

it is 6 a.m.
the sub is to be junked at 9.

CONSTANCE HILLS

TWO GIRLS IN A SWING

I
abroad the cold sea, continents,
paper trees and lanterns
fold them here, hung
in shafts of choice, gondola
rocked over sweet grass bent
with bite of tenderness.
Straw-sweetly the dyed bird sings,
sweet the china dolls sleep on
their arm, their laugh
cough of stone thrown in well of wind
sweet grass between their teeth, tongue
bitter choke-cherry chalked.

74

the narrow stroke divides
oak-sieved suns burning on the green,
under woodbine ruffles coaxes
vixen eyes awake;
cradled east, cradled west,
large hands crammed in worsted
fate, empty of sermon, they breathe
rusty mist hearing the channel flood
break on the revetment
of their learning.

ARLINGTON

withered halloos
      charge and course
across the graces, grass and stone;
candy childhood skyrockets
blue, red, where
two birds drown and cease
in even void.
flowers are flags. So many
flowers, not mud-spotted,
new, as if hooraying July four
from children's hands, wave
one rule length each above
his ground.
      White geometric stones
fly by (so much stone is used
to tell so much) aptly
whirl tic tac toe into eyes
behind eyes, done
      filmed
          microfilmed.
Pure is stone,
undefiled by rage, O,
it doesn't make me sad, the
old woman said, (there were
too many at hand for argument)
Do you cry for someone?
For the unprideful stone, for shades
of hell mud carries on their shoes.
You cry for too many, she said,
going. The trees
bellow out a crypt vacuity (no
sense wasting the traveler's summer)
      cough, chew gum, swear, call

'dear' across the river.
Make Be be
      Been
         Microfilmed.
O, Potomac, constant in memorial weather
hush battle cries
be tears,
     be stone,
mother

ROBERT EARL HODGE, JR.

A SONG TO THE VIET CONG

I

Commend/condemn the Viet Cong,
Who've been in battle so very long,
Who for twenty years
Have defied death fears:
    From thundering super U. S. jets
        Flown by trigger-happy psychopaths;
    From in-the-name-of-God-Peace napalm showers
        That burn up huts, tots, peopled tree towers—
Done with the surgical precision
And the exacting decision
Of a frontal lobotomy—
Starting at an appendectomy.

II

Commend/condemn the Viet Cong,
Who yearn to sing the Victory Song,
Who wish that they no longer must:
    Live and die in the transient dust;
    Kill with their fathers and brothers,
    And pimp for sisters and mothers;
    Burn enemy villages;
    Commit rape and pillages;
    Submit to 19th-century cavalry treaties
        From 20th-century anti-Viet Cong-Commie yankees;
    Fix crooked Capitalist elections
        In order to vote for home-grown selections.

Refrain

People live and die
From dawn to dusk
Some live without "correct" political systems
Capitalism, Communism, and other isms
Sheepherders fight for the right to own the sheep
Even if some are maimed, lamed, or put to sleep.

76

BABY JESUS

Baby Jesus
Cried in the manger
Woke the neighbors
Each a stranger,
Who bore gifts,
                fresh and new,
For the Holy baby Jew
To quiet the brat just born
So the donors could sleep till morn.

Baby Jesus —
Holy-skinned,
Holy-eyed,
Holy-genitaled Jesus —
Sucked
        fresh milk from
His mother's sore tit,
And He belched,
Babbled and drooled.

Joseph said:
My son's going to grow up
To be a King
Or a Savior.

ONE DAY I SAW THE POPE STANDING ON A HILL

One day I saw the Pope standing on a hill;
He wore his golden robes, bore his shiny staff
And stood straight and almost still
For about an hour and a half;
He immersed the jelly rabble—
Little hungry birds stretching their beaks for food—
With spiritual promises and other holy babble
And blasted the lewd, shrewd, and half-nude
And solaced the dead and those bereft;
Then the Pope   up
            pulled   his pants
                            and
                                left!

D. HOLLAND

EXILE

The days are moving much too quickly now
And I cannot remember all the times past
There is a hurt and a cold wind
A feeling something loved will soon be lost
A laugh, a voice, a cry

A touch

A remembered line filled with visions
Of dark shadows, longed for
A special day
A special night
Dancing through a momentarily forgotten present
Hate forgotten, a hope unfulfilled
Minds torn and tears turned to clouds
Beauty sought and found; pain endured
Sometimes alone
Warmth and cold in a same-single moment
Time — alone in silence to heal the mind
Times together in stark involvement
White light terror and death-dark sound
A name replaced by a new face
A wound repaired and scar hidden
A small bird passes away and so too a sight, a sound
A summer

EXILE II

I remember North Beach at night
The darkness inches from my eyes
Yet thousands of lights
All kinds; all colors
Individual specks
Dotting each inch of storefront,
Coffeehouse, sideshow
Lounge, chinadell

Noise
Noise of cars
People
Jerk and Swim from every door

78

And down a sidewalk
Stumbling with momentum and roach
A youngboy scared
Tripped beyond the limit
Talking with his gods
I stand and watch
And tell my friend
Sally'll find him and that'll be that

At the Condor I think about entering
Through the sidewalkcafewindows
But I don't think they would
Like me in their place
And we pass the Spanish joint
That Eloy loves
And the walkup with a Keaneface
In the window

We investigate an alley
Wide as a boulevard
With no lights
And no purpose

And the Palace
With its dark glasses
And dark classes
And beautiful minds
Breaking out everywhere
The nervous cool
Big as a Stopsign
Upstairs the prisonhotel
Which always turned me off
A labyrinth of passages
And voices from locked doors
Where Park lived
And wandered; inhaling the
Sweetair and
Shooting #9
"My God, Sara,
You always look neat."
"Yeh, well — ."
Patpathair

79

I REMEMBER

I would tell him:
"Come, let's get out of here
Let me take you
Out. Let's see beautiful
Things."
But he could see the church
From his window
And his friends could visit him
And he could dig the
Whole world from his room
With his needle
And Tinkerbell, who was ill
Quite a bit

So I would leave, and
It would be a
Sunnysunday, quiet and
The N.B. dwellers
Would be out walking the
Habit and gossiping
And sterilizing their amphetamined
Bodies in the sunlight
Sunglasses to hide the dilated
Holes

I have brunch with Jose
At the Cat, because
It's Sunday and the afternoons are
Long and quiet in the
Beach and the Sundaysettingsun
Makes me nervous and the
Lord'sdaynight is quieter here
And the coolones are harder
To find in bunches
So I hit a movie or
Go to bed

POEM

A woman came to me in my sleep
"Come," she said to me
"Come to the mourning place
Come mourn with us, for my husband
                                    is
                                        dead."

80

She wore a black veil,
And I whispered in her ear,
"My father died day before yesterday."
Her sorrow and my sadness became one
"Ah, let us be sad for all,
                    come then
To the mourning place, here.
Here is your pillow."

I knelt on the carpeted steps and laid
My head on the pillow and cried
For I missed my father very much

Then abruptly I arose and left
The mourning place for
                    I had to tell
My friend
My father is dead.

NANCY HOLLAND

fifth floor walkin' up room
with slanted up ceiling, red orange
carpet an' all else in a mystic display
of chaotic beauty.
window looks out onto shingled roof &
other uncurtained bare wonderful dormers —
who wonders there? i sleep.
guitar case in corner, someone standing
at an alcove mirror, water bubbling
in the sink, gold sunlight ghastly pale
faces early morning will turn them.
table full of junk & caps & keys &
someone's posties & who cares for
it; it's a nice room in Genève &
how nice wouldn't it be if only
i could see my fareyed great thought
young beloved
watches me from the other little bed.
shambles an' color an' things all
rush to claim the morning,
an' me, o god as well
ivanov, i love you.

GARY HOTHAM

The cool grass was fresh.
And they come and come to stay.
My grass is hot black.

This morning was bright —
No worries, No troubles — Then.
Midmorning is black.

Away to a land.
A long way from home today.
In the soil now.

And there he stood — all.
Facing the morning sun — rise.
And he went onward.

I will not now know —
Your mind is in disorder.
I can see your moves.

Snow was on the ground.
The air was cold with freezing.
wind. Hot with anger.

ROBERT HUGHES

LAMENTATION

"'Tis bitter cold, and I am sick at heart"
Screams from hollow, hungry eyes
Dragging sullen mouths and bodies
Along well planned barren walks
Is this modern limbo
The time of warmth and brightness
Wished for half a century ago
We don't work in sweatshops

Just worry over golf scores
Am I the sacred oak
Of druids of old
Planted in a comfortable lawn
By a woman in pink shorts
Or do I mistake some streetlamp
For the evening star of Venus?

STREET SCENES

In the automats people cry
The spaghetti is cold and limp
The englassed jelly doughnut
Torments little boys
It's real though
The center has no seeds
Eucharistic broken bread peers out
It's too stale and old to take anyway
The sign says
"Untouched by Human Hands"

An old lady carries another sign
"Cannonize Ben Franklin"
Pentecost occurred in Pennsylvania
As the electric dove
Leapt from the sky to a key
Giving divinity to machines

Americans, you are so ingenious
Your crosses, even burning ones
Do not twist
Nietzsche is dead
Superman, the anti-villain,
Appeared in the comics in 1939

Arrogant university ologists
Over coffee and cigarettes
Somewhere in the neon nirvana
Discuss the origin
And purpose of it all
Oblivious to the answer at the next table
Where a man sits
With his head in his hands
Somehow Mr. Darwin's missing link
Mr. God's Adam
Imagined death

THE HIGH PRIEST OF MYSTERY

In the satin time
Of equinox melt and bud
An old man sat on a bench
His fingers dancing like crab legs
Tickled by nervous sands
In this spring he saw
No sniffing dogs or flower draped girls
But heard the cracking ice
Shattering winter's shroud
Cold times ago he wrapped himself
Around warm basement pipes
Seeing in the safety of sherry dreams
Golden and silver apples
Snakishly hidden behind
His pitchfork veined eyes

Children in the earth born grass
Feared his gaze or touch
He feared to stir or see
His hairy nerved bones
Echoed on the mud and straw
Beneath the still lake
A high priest of mystery
He kept a moaning vigil
With bullfrogs who sang
When fragrant blossoms fell
Into the water's wild green ooze
Into muck as heavy
As an old man's sorrows
Or fertile as angel's tears
He wondered about night's
Creeping and crawling things

The children that night
Their innocence fogged
Heard his whisper
And saw his face
Amidst the night silhouetted leaves
They prayed for the dawn

RUTHERFORD JAMES

ALONENESS IS A PROFOUND NIGHT

Hail! admirable being perched on a suspension bridge
    stretched between two cliffs of imperturbable asphalt-harshness.
Pilgrim is come wondering on the dark path
      to search for candor flickering like lance-match,
         only hotter.
It burns with waving fronds of undulating feelings
      never clearly expressed
         but always violent in a slow, sure way;
He, the traveller, is greeted by all
        the knights of the days' ending;
like a rubber waterfall stretching until
        elasticity is but a mockery of what
          could have been eternity. —

the figure, slowly with age, moves from the middle
    of the bridge and past the chasm until
the sun on the plain green greets him,
    painted red the skylight in the morning
        gives no suggestion of nature without passion.
he moves again to the place where the light
        is earliest.

He, taking with him a little of the sun's blood-red
    substance, so that some may know that his
play day of sanguinity is genuinely an uttered response
    of the furred bear, naked on the fireplace's hearth —
      a rug to be stepped upon is instead becoming
        foundation of evening after, —

He, with black folds of robe draped
      ever gaunt, thin, bent, ascetic frame,
        crucified against the pain,
    must feel of having spoken so often,
      so evenly, so reasonably
        being all the while ignored, —
and with red light fading across the face,
      eyes rapidly becoming ashes —
    empty, gaping in tired skull;

        there is a short clipped laugh,
      then, silence   and
        finally, against a dark sky,
      a flash of a comet.

a first thing is an austere creation
  out of the endless caused beginnings
comes an hesitant indeterminacy muttered
softly so as not to detract from the bread, purple ribbon
of fate's Girth which binds the skies
    to the earthly loans of finite certainty;

the anathema of the unhegelian essence
  crouched upon a pad
  of a pond at dawn waiting —
in grey light that hangs upon the willows
  like a damp mantle
  shooting luna's reign
    with streaks of predetermined light.
    pausing in this instant to sing
      praises of phaeton, the sun stealer.

the uncanny web spun of a thousand spiders
    who did not know one another's names
but could write with webs
  an ode to Arachne, the recipient of noble Athene's wrath . . .
    with such spinnings, mention is made
      of a burnished pattern
      crept there under the fates' thimble.

with hesitation, i construct
  an image of uterine creatures,
    folded into illusions of half-life,
   wound into gestures of uncomprehending
hollowness,
      pretending in their bent forms
    no meaning but that of
   empty sheets thrown over
   the invisible creature
     drifting through no-time
   capturing in its mistaken analogy
cryptic mutterings of unprepared monasteries
    waiting, then, for the entrance
of the mendicant sinner who will forgive himself
    for his own identity, and
    perhaps for a moment's time already flown past
      will rise upon a metaphor

to see an allegory
    more than half-conceived
        not dependent upon a sun's rising
from its own bed
    to make it tomorrow —
        then, it is what it is that causes
            words to be thrown ambiguously
                on a lined page,
    it is with this gesture
                that i become, at once,
                    and at another time
                        a poet.

HOBART JARRETT

APPLES

Slithering upright
balancing steady
giddy, slipping
horizontal —
then up, upright
python-feet tall:
he hissed (embarrassing)
ambiguity;
forthrightly he spat out
his brand of vacuity.

I made the grade, O Fearful Eve.
Sensibly, you can take reprieve:
From there to here and up to there.
None but the brave can taste the fare.

She tasted. Giddy, she arose,
Activating a box of timeless woes.

Slithering upright
panthering unsteady
(movements designed
to make a man heady),
she balanced
vertical.
I was enticed
to taste the fruit;
un-Adam I

87

I failed to do it.
She hissed
she slithered
Eve-feet tall.
I thought of him
before the fall.

COMMUNICATION

No word nor sound nor utterance
  was ever able to acquire
  the faintest simulation dim
  of what my soul and I desire.

We would but tell, so you could feel,
  the strength and beauty that are ours:
  the magnitude which we become
  when in the contemplative hours

We think of you.

DEPARTURE

Thundrous engines
  all noises silenced —
  save the spluttering, stuttering,
  deviled staccato
  of engines themselves
  which belch forth flames!

Uneven as the trapping
  sound of the motors,
  the misbeat thumping
  of my untuned being
  sickened and sank —
  by the mechanism sickened.

It was a bastard plane
  that God had to love!

For what seemed an hour
  (a matter of minutes)
  I watched in silence
  the blinking retreat
  of the soaring demon
  with its angelic cargo.

ROBERTA L. JENNINGS

RUSH STREET

It is hot — very hot. The street below is sweating with hot cars and hot people. A white, stuffy smog hangs over the tops of the city's skyscrapers. It is the kind of day that makes you want to head for the nearest air-conditioned bar and feel the coolness of a gin and tonic or a touch of cold beer trickle down your throat. But it is still early and the bars are not yet opened.

When the heat beats down in the early morning, it is a sign for all the locals to stretch their limbs and yawn, their heads hurting from the hangover left over from last night's heavy drinking and partying. Slowly some emerge into the morning heat to work, to wash, to wander and wonder, knowing and not particularly caring, that it is another day. The street becomes alive with the honking, screeching, swimming cars, Hondas, bicycles. The sidewalks hum with the unsteady beat of tennis shoes, heels, sandals.

Sitting silent, listening to a soft radio in a near-northside apartment, far above the teeming street, we can see the seeming madness flowing through the Area, stretching out toward the beautiful buildings of the Loop and the beach, already crowded.

People wander about aimlessly, too lazy even to think; several have taken the day off from work. At two o'clock the bars will open and we will go to "The Zoo" for a drink; at four the swimmers will appear for a beer or two; at six the workers, after their "hard day at the office", will come; at nine we'll all be there: The drinkers, the runners, the seekers, the funners, the boozers, the choosers, the makers and the made. This being Friday night, the Street will be jammed with the proud and damned, the rough and tough and meek and weak seeking a soul or a song, wanting a break or a make.

Some will rush unhesitantly from bar to bar to pub while others will wait. Sit and wait, not knowing for what, but waiting, always waiting. Hoping their vigil will be rewarded. Then finally trudging to a home that is not a home and their empty, empty beds. While others, who could not wait, laugh or moan in the night-beds of the City, until their desire becomes limp and their lust is no longer heavy upon them.

And somewhere a pinpoint of fire may flicker for a moment and die, as a Rudy-on-a-fire-escape lights a cigarette, or as a lone girl on Oak Street beach sheds tears of remorse and sets fire to her regret. And the cry deep within the memory's soul will make an old man toss briefly in sleep while a drunken, ageless, sexless being sways softly at the corner of Rush and Elm to an old, old song.

Loud laughter and dancing come from an all night party as young couples-for-a-night swear and gulp and press against each other, arms and legs entwined, breast against naked chest, in a last effort to render the night unwasted — in a last protest to the coming morning. And then sleep to the first dawn of a new day, passed out in a peaceless, restless sleep.

This is life here on the Street, never stopping in its mad screaming pace, and never really getting anywhere either. If things seem too hard to bear, there's always Rush Street. If there is nothing for which to care, there's always the Area. If vital questions remain unanswered there's always Irving's, The Store, the Zoo. If you have problems there's always Easy Street, Catfish, the Lodge.

Come one, come all! Feel the call, the pull, the sucking of the Street! "Give me your tired, your poor, your huddled masses, yearning to be free!" You won't be free, you won't solve any problems. But live it up while you're on the road down and you'll have one crazy bitch of a time doing it! No matter how many mornings disturb you — you will still have the nights — the wild, raucous nights — to wallow in and exclude all else.

There is a feel about the place that is like a creeping cloud always a few steps behind, but gaining. It will encompass you and feed off you unless you are strong. If you are strong, this grey non-life feeling may not hit you too hard — you may not notice it at all. But with every beer you drink, a little of it seeps into your veins and soon your "just a few evenings of fun" becomes a way of life. Why create, why study, why take time out to be great, when you can sit warmly with "the group" and drink or dance. Hail to Rush Street! Hail to the "Conquering Worm!"

THE SPIES

I despise the guys who are spies in disguise
Because they surmise we are wise to their disguise
It is time to arise and take them by surprise
Before they utilize their whole enterprise.

They drop from the skies with a gleam in their eyes
Advertising their lies and thinking they're wise.
The head of the spies is after the Prize
And despises the guys who would dare compromise.

"What is the prize?" exclaim the spies.
"A plan to advertize," number One spy replies.
"Epitomize!" number Five spy cries.
So he tries to comprise the plan of his devise.

90

A hush fell over the group of spies
As their leader began to eulogize.
With whispered cries and flashing eyes
He commences the plan of his devise.

"We've escaped the incise, we've eluded the excise.
"We have a bloody good form of exercise.
"We brutalize. We terrorize.
"And if we can't do it right, we improvise.
"So now, my fraternizing spies, I think it's time we televise."

"We'll televise!" arise the cries
"And dramatize the roles of spies,
"And make a profit of enormous size."

"Man from U.N.C.L.E., F.B.I.'s,
"Secret Agents, Private Eyes,"
Say some of the spies, and another one cries,
"I'll 'Get Smart', and satirize."

To summarize this page of lies
Of how I despise the spies in disguise,
I'll just say I was smart not to medicinize,
Because how many words rhyme with "Kildare"?

While ships do reel
in Saturn steel of loveliness
of boundlessness
of hypo-homeless soundlessness
now night now black
now white suzak
of overturned voluminous
and calling out come hither thus
the while coliniquy or two
sail thru the open voyam

We're homeless in our heads and beds
while domelessness the skylark treads
and out the heat beat reet of heart
goes soul of slumber
wrapped in lumber
dragging oh so dead.

Forgive me love for I have sinned
Perhaps I'll die with night's next wind
And all the siren sounds of San Francisco
will mean naught.
If death so bold this hand should hold
and cold galls mold my breast to gold
Remember that was you I told
I loved my life-long best.

So rest, so rest. Within my chest
of treasure is a memory nest
and there we laugh and there we sing
and wing away a world of spring
and sigh a song of summer Sun
so long a distance I have come —
so long a span of time.

So out we sail to break the gale
Through night we reel in ships
        of Saturn steel.

JEFF JENSEN

DUST

He read everything,
Everything good
Trying to learn
As best he could.

He's dead now
So's his dog
And all is dust.

Hours he spent thinking,
Thinking why
Trying to find
The linking tie.

He's dead now
So's his dog
And all is dust.

To dust he never,
Never looked
And there his
Answer has been booked.

He's dead now
So's his dog
Volume, infinity,
Page uncertain.

ALICIA JONES

A PLEA FOR INSANITY

Why should I stay
            in this world?

Where everything around
            calls out loud for the
                blood of my people.

Better, to stay here
            safe
    in my own world.

Here
I need not fear anguish.
All controversy is mine.
Only
Loneliness
Calls to me for mercy,
While love peters persistently
            through my blood in
            a sad sightless path.

Yet —
        there are those who call me
            coward.

And —
Deep within
I feel the
Desire
To shout to all mankind,
Let me be but a man!
But then,
I know
Fear —
Still will I proclaim —
I will be a man!
        if not in this world,
            in mine own.

93

EARL JONES

ODE TO A DARK HERO

(Felipe, slave to Simon Bolivar in
Colombia's War for Independence)

A coward say you me, my lord?
He whispered softly through the foam
That bloodied cheek and chest and valiant steed.

    A coward, sire? And hand unstaunched
    The gaping wounds that dealt
    By ball and sword had death to him decreed.

A coward, no, my lord and leige,
I sprang to fore as want of yore
To be *the first*, the charge to lead.

    They shot me through, o master, sir,
    I'm riding dead but could not go
    Without one glimpse of him I loved,
    One farewell touch to plead.

Then down he plunged, a soddened heap
Of him that through the mem'ried years
Of battle-ridden liberation wars
Had served the devil, man, and god
Through grief contained and conquered fears.

    He bore him up, no stone to bruise
    In Andes snows, in jungle strife;
    He brought him food, his thirst he quenched;
    He warmed him, cheered him, clothed his flesh;
    He nurture was, companion, too;
    Though two, they shared one life.

Ex-slave this black-skinned gift
To grand Colombia's hero came
Hell-charged in battles, bitter fought,
And rightly earned, *the first*, his name.

    The Royal troops this night-black savage feared.
    With shouts, invectives foul he sped
    Their souls to hell and bodies cleft
    With cold steel slashing trunk from head.

But battles end; the trumpet blown
And back he trod, the demon flown,
Now in its place a touch, a tone
That soothed the pain, the mental moan
Of him who ordered, death had sown.

Then uniforms he smooths and shines
By firelight toils til tasks are done
While warming, watching
Guards his own — his master, father, son.

So you guard, too; his vigil keep
This revered saint of fire and heart.
Pray, sons of Venezuela's plain
That he might strength impart.

For God so loved this swarthy one
He greater love and valor gave
And diademed his sacrifice
With hallowed, hero's grave.

FISHERMEN GLIMPSED AT COQUIMBO *(Chile)*

Slish, there the fisher boat hastens
Cross wet sand to its berth in the sea
Brown backs tensed, muscles glint in the sunlight
Heaving chest, eve tide calls, float her free.

Row her hard! Ride the wave! Be the first there!
Yonder penguins pursuing their prey
Mark the school's traversed path, there must we go
Ere the sun robes its face, hides the day.

Cold is the jet black sea bosom
Nets grope in her unfathomed green
Klok, sounds a distant friend's oarlock
Flicker fire, inner felt, seldom seen.

Pips on the world's outer rimlet
Lined up in illusion's neat row
Dividing sky's star-splattered darkness
From fish-jewelled depths just below.

Wheeling gulls clarinet their returning
Caterwauling demand their gilled share
Yelping pups, fishwife shrieks, offsprings' whistles —
Welcome clamor befriends dawn's bright air.

Acclaim the prize ray, shark and rock bass!
Gut them out, fold wet nets, beach the carvel
Women basket finned catch to the market
Men strut home, eat their fill, then sleep well.

95

MARGARET KECK

WHY DO FLOORS CRY IN THE NIGHT

why do floors cry in the night —
and minimal exactitude fluctuate
between alternating poles
inevitably
passing through the same point
twice a generation.
the bubble ethos
will not burst yet.

RELATIONSHIP

1
Play me a mandolin chorus
on a sunken autoharp
and take me flying across
newly painted doorsteps;
wingless, I crouch beside my battered plastic horn
and watch the turpentine explode
next door to my face.

2
Driving through plantations
all of them — us
screech — freak out
grating noise to unskilled ants' feet.

3
Defiant boredom
breeding self-exhalting misery
gone in a go away quadrangle
with me and dog and
aching hearts full of
run fever;
      two blades of grass — touching
      bend to each other
      yours breaks
gentle soft soft laugh touch.

4
Orange lit intensity
smoky mindless mindful
soul grope . . .

5
I love you

6
Wind freeing balsam wind
screaming
raping away false eyelashes and
maple sugar breath . . .
7
Soft harsh fullness
fifteen the world in a
pretended stable and
music drawing inward and
universe in me fullness . . .
8
Pride no yes no yes
no yes no yes
i love you yes
no
9
Bleeding sidewalk
cast off remnants of
shelter-failure trees.
10
Emptiness is.
11
I love you oh yes
12
i love you.
13
Harsh grating lack of
inert nobility
black ringing hanging wall phone
god is dead
death is forever and so is the past
14
smile wave
        once a week hi awkward
        paper airplanes showering
        onto crushed burned matchbooks
        and cream cartons . . .
15
i love you
16
How long?
hallucinations —
unforgotten fantasies
play games at midnight.

i want to see unicorns
playing hopscotch on barstools
running steeplechases
in abandoned graveyards
knocking over tombs
i want to clap for
any menial thing
that's different
and shines without
aluminum foil coating
i want to cry on my birthday
and run races over chairtops
and fly — fly on rooftops
and parachute through the
aurora borealis
to meet the unicorns
for breakfast
in my basement.

TERRY KIHARA

the sunset hues in violet,
color fog clouds caught in
the green of a tree, away.
the lace moss embracing the branches,
felled by heavy rains,
moved by incessant winds.
beneath a wall of stone, the sea,
a deathly beauty in the worn sea's wave,
sounds gainst the cold rock shore.
white foam, broken into bizarre patterns.
cliff rocks rise from the water,
drowned by her wetness,
bathed in her salt mist.
gulls lowly, highly above her crests;
the sky lifts out of the sea.
away far a shore... sand, for birds to rest,
for shells to die . . .

A. MacT. KINNAIRD

TINT LUVE

1

I see ye nou the wey ye were thon nicht —
Sae braw, sae snod — my, whit a bonnie sicht, wi'oot a doot.
    An' me sae prood wi'oot a care.
I never even held yer han'; I thocht it wisna richt — oor first
    Nicht oot, but there'd be mony mair.

2

I saw ye tae yer door. Says I, "Guid nicht.
I'll tak ye oot the morn, gin that's a'richt." An you said,
    "Ay." An' syne it stertit on tae rain.
I didna hae a coat. Ye gied me yours. I looked a fricht. — It
    Kep' me dry. 'Twis better faur nor nane.

3

I daundert hame, yer coat aboot me ticht.
The nicht wis derk an' driech; ma step wis licht; ma hert wis
    Gled. An' aye I thocht on you a lot,
An' as I thocht, I cried masel' a fule; but ere that nicht I
    Gaed tae bed, I took an' kissed yer coat.

4

Niest day, 'twis sic a bonnie efternune
As frae the toun barefit we wandert in like bairnies twa.
    An' later on, I held yer han'
As tae thon meikle rock we run, the bonnie loch abune.
    I gaed awa' nae mair a laddie, but a man.

5

Gin I forget a' ailse, I'll aye min' this:
The thirlin' rapture o' thon first sweet kiss. Ye were ma ain.
    An' my, we gat sae close
Wi'in thae twa-'hree weeks thegither spent — whit went amiss
    That nou ye're gaen? For, Losh, ma hert is boss.

6

Ye gaed awa'; ma hert wis like tae brak.
A lad oot-bye an' you were unca pack, an' weel I kent
    Ye'd be wi' him an' mindna me.
Niest day I wrote tae ye; short syne I gat yer letter back:
    Ma luve wis tint. Alas! It couldna be.

THE OLD WOMAN WHO SWALLOWED A GNAT
(Scribes & Pharisees — which strain out a gnat & swallow a camel)

There was an old woman who swallowed a gnat.
Fancy that:
To swallow a gnat.
    But a gnat is so small
    It won't harm her at all.

There was an old woman who swallowed a camel.
That's a rather big mammal
To swallow — a camel.
    She swallowed the camel; then gargled and spat.
    And would you believe it? She coughed up the gnat.
But she just left the camel.
She didn't give damn all.
        Just left it inside,
        And soon after, she died.

(This story to mind the comparison brings
How with care we observe the most trivial things;
    While the great things we miss.
    — Have done with all this!
        Let the lesson be painted in brilliant enamel:
        "Don't strain out a gnat and then swallow a camel.")

VIET NAM

Dead!
A tiny baby, hid for safety underneath a bed.
    A hand-grenade was hurled.
The mother holds his bloody blackened head
    And shrieks her agony to all the world.

Burned:
A leper hospital. The callous fighter-pilot spurned
    To note the scarlet cross.
A shelter once, 'tis now but rubble churned;
    And flesh and blood, but smould'ring heaps of dross.

Why?
Vile slaughter, indiscriminate and crude. The children die,
    The villages are bombed.
Democracy and freedom? — This the lie
    'Neath which a nation's honour lies entombed.

Peace!
A docile, servile state, maintained in order by police,
    For business int'rests sure?
No! A state wherein oppressions cease
    And people stand alone and rest secure.

100

VIRGINIA GRACE KNIGHT

He has come back to me:
What wayward wind blew him here,
    If for only a second —
Laugh, lying lips!
Tell him not you love him still —
    Lest he be blown away
On the breath
Of your whisper . . .

DOROTHY KOBAK

IF MY LOVE WERE HERE

If my love were here
I would reach out
And touch his hand
Suddenly — without any reason
Except to remind him
That every moment is full of him.

If my love were here
I would bend close
And whisper "I love you"
Suddenly — without any reason
Except that my passion cannot be contained.

If my love were here
I would call him a tender name
Not only "darling" or "my beloved"
But something new — unvoiced by any other
The leitmotiv for *my* special love.

If my love were here
I would be so good to him
Easily — knowing just how
Because to see him happy and at peace
Would fully quench the only thirst I know.

If my love were here
I would be complete
Not finished — but eager for life
Breathless for more of it!
Awaiting each dawn to find and savor him again.

101

ALMOST AT YOUR SIDE

Two steps behind is almost at your side.
I stay enough apart, so I can quickly hide
A vagrant tear,
A flagrant fear,
When you must say goodbye.

Two steps behind is almost at your side.
You move enough ahead, to span the ocean wide.
To mark a sight,
Then climb a height,
And so you smile goodbye.

But avidly, I hurry fast,
To link our arms and laugh at last —
We do not part!
You have my heart!
I do not hear goodbye.

J. ROBERT KONDRICK

MIST

The school-yard clatters with sounds of recess.
I search among the scrawny limbs and scabbed
Knees for the cream puff I've been holding
In my mouth since the sun cracked its first smile.

Are they real? Flowing dresses and pre-kept faces
Staring at me in bewilderment. Braces flash in
The sun. Mid-day. Time for play: Our future
Leaders at tag and what-not.

"You are the American future!" I was told this my
First morning. "The nation grovels at your feet!"
(pause)

Mist shrouds the memory of the painful. The past
Concealed by waterfalls, Screams, Its throat hoarse
Of laughter. Dreams, like ketchup bottles, leap
And splatter from the shelf into a thousand weary

Moron jokes. You have taken my hand and led me
To a valley of darkness. Here, you say, is a home
For the ages. The shadows will comfort you. I
Lay and waited for death, comfortable Talons to

Shred and rid me of flesh. The angel Oz hovered
Near, frightened. Lichen crusts the walls, and
Drops blamelessly at my feet. You gave me a
Companion, an actress of your stage. We ground

102

Laughed, and frightened of the Echo called
It love. The third act is a fading memory.
Blackness sheathes me. I wait in silence.

(end of pause)

A regimental bell clashes against innocuous
Laughter. They are called to their studies.
I am left alone,
Alone and wondering . . .

MARKET STREET —LAVENDER

I took the night off to see
you — waited a year. Wanting
to delve into your warm
mysteries. I stood-clutched in midnight
(12th & Market was cold in '66). Waiting
to taste your unveiled lips
to hold you under me
                        — moaning   thrashing   mine

(were you at the library?hung up?busy? — that year)

The night we found our bodies — first night — we
met, faces painted for Saturday, neon
crashing, above us, flashing. Drinks & smiles exchanged — the
meaningless books we had read.
More liquor
            Later in a faded motel room — hashish — Morning —
awareness harsh — in wondering naked lines
we parted.
        Later — our eyes-in real —
                we met touched & loved

                                Tonight
under flashing stop-lites waiting — loving you
impossibilities fled — I count the stars successfully
I explore my hands —
Palms that shaped you — fingers having molded you — now
cold, bare, alone —

                                    Last
cigarette falls — a home found on cold gray
slabs, I leave   — wanting
                        yet
embraced
        by your mystery

103

POEM

Do
I
pick my nose
&
eat
the green
because I'm self sustaining? —
or
merely
a pig — ?

FROM THE ARMCHAIR A FLICKER

My wife believes my analyst is of noble lineage,
The analyst thinks my wife is overworked,
I believe he's screwing her on the sly.

I sit at home — a restless night —
Waiting for the stockmarket to
Drag its feet thru my cellar.

Ulcers stem from hypertension. My
Doctor expresses wisdom in milligrams.
Three weeks per annum I am allowed rest.

Behavior pattern gone haywire!
My son smokes marijuana for security —
I just smoke and burp

My home is an amphitheater for Soupy Sales.
I tour the world with sugar bosoms,
And sleep in their cleveage image.

In my youth I scrambled for dollars,
Now eggs on my wife's tired days.
Communism? Can no longer define it.

Who do I blame? Myself? — Sundays only!
The million identical brothers who
Walk-Look-Talk-Drink and Vomit

In the mirror? Perhaps the Grand
Canyon for being so damn grand? No-one?
(don't look now hollywood) perhaps people

Are only People!?///

POEM

Only possible conclusions
From silicon injected minds
      dangle
      before
      me
They wait
      wait
      wait
      wait — for programed acceptance.
Globes
      of self sustaining utopia —
(on them, secretly, I breakfast.
      They bring nausea, sharpening-ripening
me for their death. I unclothe — leap naked
      into life — into dawn, passion intense —
into twilight — into shadows . . .)
      I vomit - wretch - & freed,
          go on —

SAINT CHARLES: TERMINAL

it is AM at the bus stop
morning cold and nervous
dawn has not yet crept from the sea
I cannot blame it. chattering teeth
huddle close for warmth

the waitress scratches and serves coffee
cigarettes are consumed
lips chapped and calloused tear at the paper.
I linger with the strained sheets of laughter
from the girls of the corner

if I signal they will come. the
night is perilous. fate a talon suspends
from the ceiling I cannot defy the claw
in my brain. I wait then laugh
louder and louder until my thunder

shakes the counter and tips and change
clatter to the floor. tourists stare
coffee flows from cup to table. I laugh.
tears blind me I rise then silent and
brush my clothes. I leave a dime though

I drank nothing. no-one speaks.
I leave startled faces.
The night waits crashing . . .

MARCEL KSHENSKY

GRAND FINALE

In darkness illumination
merry moon whispering winds
to stars glittering bathing in black
meteor descending onto
plain

bodies scattered
dyed grass filled with mourners
for innocent dead,
the tears flow
tonight

unleashed sky
carefully showering
rice paddies
only food to destroy
      "no humans will die
      we shall drop leaflets
      in advance"
they shall wait for death to come from heaven

silently the tears trickle
across hollow cheeks
the tears glittering
bathing in red
the meteors fall no more

MARY LASKY

DUNES

Before Us!

Behind Us!

Loom the Giants of the Earth. Merrily we frolic on their bosoms.
They — grateful for company — jestfully tickle our bronze toes
with granular fingertips. Now that we have come, they raise their
walls of stillness enclosing us fast within.

Night Descends!

Sinking deeper into golden waters, we stand captured prisoners
of Beauty. Our hearts ascend to join a wayward gull in his song
of praise.

Mists of Morn
Once more surround us with the turbulence of *man*.
Yet
The memory of sand palaces embeds itself deeply into our
souls, quenching our thirst for freedom.

DAVID LAWSON

THE TURNING

Meadows at dawn
Once lent to us an air
Of fond abstraction,
Framed as we ever were
By symbols strutting
From a boundless past —
Parading archetypes,
Eidetic moons,
Clandestine ponds
Of fragile sound untuned.

Silent as sod
The animus of hills
Advanced, descending through
Young rivers of our personhood,
Touching the roots,
Caressing earthen grooves,
Noetic winds
In cock-crow overtures
Strumming the cobbled
Alleys of our minds.

Naked as stems
We grew away from things,
Fixed boundaries in time
While bright projections
Showered the broken
Reservoirs of years
With altered images.
Lost in an age
Of whispering mentality,
With thinking reeds
As harps unstrung,
We came to grieve
The death of elders,
Confessed in solemn riddles,
Witnessed the birth of cities.

107

GIRLS IN THE SEVENTIES

Though dust conceals
my loves these photos span
my mantelpiece,
my silent river is
my memory,
whose owner ever ran
from door to door,
the brownstone kingdom his.

Here I, the scion
of what homeless home
and nebulous
and nameless name did search
on nervous feet
in shoes too cheap to roam
to say, there is no God,
there is no Church.

though i would say
there is a girl who may
when she should come
before she goes this spring
from maryland or texas
she will stay
and we shall love manhattan
we shall sing

night will be communion
our days will glow
we bear children
of our enterprise
so meaningful
the rhythm and the quiet flow
and thus
our struggle turns victorious

what hopes will blossom
what delirium
undreamt-of pageant
which surpasses all
imaginings
our kingdom it has come
it has been done on earth
how epical . . . !

The seventies were far and wide,
my girls
have come and gone to cry,
their faces fresh
from other places,
searching girls where swirled
the tide of nights and days,
experiments in flesh.

DEATH IN THE WEST

He was a secret poet, sped his art
Down highways of the night low-beamed, aloof
To shoulders, medians; by sage-brush switched
No signals, splintered where his blood was ditched.

From dusk at Shasta following the way
Of extirpation, hunched in Oregon
(The wheel exacts a twilight toll on limbs)
Then bearing for the Badlands failed to see

The wrath of critics mounting on the hills,
Nor gave a sign he knew that works are judged
(Some momentary loss of prescience)
Which darkly move with cosmic arrogance

Beyond the tolerance of roads for life
Or art to suffer cancellations dealt
On desert, bluff or mesa — swift as birds
That circle to observe the death of words.

MARGARET ANN LAZENBY

CYCLE

The darkened heavens grumble overhead,
As heavy, somber clouds their warnings toll.
They're telling of the strength that we might dread,
For who knows if destruction be their goal?

As streaks of power flash across the sky,
I fear to feel the press of storm; and then
I wonder what has made the heavens cry.
Will all the world ne'er be bright again?

Yet these celestial tears are not so cursed,
For they are falling gently and seem gay
To be the means of quenching nature's thirst
In such a wondrous and dramatic way.

A rainbow is in view; and far from sad,
The sun is coming out. The earth is glad.

DEBORAH LEWIS

I got
those chills
again today,
everlasting
cutting
carefully,
centering,
up and down my spine
and well,
hell, honey
I just hollered
because they came
from way down deep
down deeper
and deeper
still

and I know
now
that when they come
again
I won't be able to
carry that cold
any longer.
and they're going to come again.

I thought maybe
you ought to know.

TERRENCE LISBETH

MR. NOBODY'S SHOP

Tipping tangent to an expanding circle:

He punches time cards in London,
   listens to silver coins exchanged for
     Venus of the Pawn Shop Window,
and in the attic of coffee cups and pealed light bulbs,
the scribe interprets this sect, that,
falling shouts into Florentine villas.

The fanatic, a shout, another war.
A shot, Franz Ferdinand, and the china breaks.

SUZANNE LISTER

IN CONTINUANCE, AGAIN

Still . . .
   Consider what yet may be
   For man's eternity fast is fading.
   Happy singing
   'Cross dark-dimmed eyes
   Brings ageless ocean
          and
   Searching sea-child
   Into everlasting Focus
   To shine a unique glory
   Upon a finite universe
   And light with warmth
   An empty, snowbound
            . . . Winter

JESSIE LITTLE

CANYON TRAIL

Veiled mountains rest against a dreaming sky;
'Neath overhanging cliff the bluebell sleeps.
Blue fields of lupine gaily shimmer by
The canyon trail that ever upward creeps.

Turn here, and suddenly the alders meet;
Deep shade and sparkling spring in ferny nook.
Pause now, and let the canyon walls repeat
Birdsong and fainter voice of chuckling brook.

Cool winds from heaven caress your weary face;
Soft checkered light erase the marks of pain.
Rest here, and let the peace of this fair place
Restore your radiant hopes and dreams again.

AUDREY LOEHR

MUTISM

New to town, I lived lonely,
Three flights up
And pursued friendship,
Returning measure for measure
Excepting hospitality
For lack of equal accomodations.

Now I live in a castle
Fine enough for my accumulated circle
Who come . . . and there is only silence.

Where are the words and the ways
I was saving for this castle
While I lived lonely,
Three flights up?

DEBBIE LOEWEN

I KNOW

i feel

the rocks cutting flesh,
beating clubs;
and
the tension inside me mounting to a furious passion.

i smell

the smoke of existence —
suffocating my soul,
and
the pungent food that is so familiar.

i see

the sectioned city,
with it's forbidding signs —
and
the fear alive in the eyes of friends.

i taste

the dirt at my door,
as it shifts to follow my life;
and
the bitterness of n'er ending tears.

i hear

the noisy chants of merciless children;
hungry for hate,
and anxious for pain.

and i know
that
i am black.

TH. JAMES LONGSHAW

FOR TASTE

Lion crouches quietly in bushes —
Heat is rising over Plain before him,
The ribbon of mountains
In the distance
Wiggles, quivers
And sways.

Lion eyes the Antelopes,
Saliva flows in
Bloody anticipation.
Crouches, crawls —
Grasses part gently,
Whisper warnings to
The Antelopes, but
The message goes unheard.
The grass parts
And Lion draws near.
Breath comes hot —

A rustle,
Lion springs —
Flash of furs,

Claws rake quivering flesh.

The herd flees,
One remains
Of bloodied fang
On gentle throat,
Of claws sunk in soft fur,
A young heart races fast;
Beats out wildly in horror.

A kill is made,
Tastes of blood.

WILLIAM E. LOVELY

the individual does not exist
say you me and every
other student, i.d., number,
and course — and he the impressive
one who never
dying will decide the fate
of life's eternal work — he
the cog, wheel, or ever what
he may be called — lists
classifies — and decides
yours, mine, and everyones
fate? — or do he say the
simple dimpled little one
with vacant blue hued
eyes (or — can't see for looking — not)
look in the basements, complexes
(the machines of age have come) and
even in the (eat, work, play, and sleep
— the evernever planner I.B.M.) last
candy machine you, she, he or I
kicked for services sake — remembers
that kick like an elephant?! and
passes through the quarter so that
other tools of man can (correct change only)
protest . . .

114

M. SCOTT MacCLELLAND

I run the beach at dawn.
I am alone with you,
The enveloping mist.
At the sundown sea
You kiss me red, then leave.
But I feel you still,
The star of eventide,
The thousand million points of energy
That heat the dark.

EDWARD A. MacPHERSON

TO THE POWERS (IF THEY BE!)

I am told that you Are, and it is enough
    For me to accept, humbly, happily . . .
    Very well — but I do not accept what I cannot believe.
To you powers then, if indeed you Be, I say:

    "Show me the way!
    I do not fear the truth!
    Show me, damn you, or I shall run amok
        For one glorious minute, and dare
            Utter with glee what otherwise
                Would be blasphemy!"

"Give me a sign, or accept my consequence:
    Freedom!
Say not that I am even a slave to the elements —
    Bah!
        The elements do not move me: I move them!
Say not that the elements
    Will one day quench me:
    Reduce me soon to driveling dotage, and then
        to shameful damnation;
    Pluck my spiteful, lonely anger from me — these
        I do not fear."

"I accept them; they may do their slavish worst.
It is you I do not accept!
    And if you would claim me, do not strike
        What you covet!
Would you pluck the flower of my reason?
    The incomprehensibility of my wonderment?
        The absurdity of my courage?!
Poor powers, you do not dare!
You would not sear the kernel and save the husk!"

THE TRESTLE

We walked that day,
   You and I (Remember?),
Walked through oft-trod streets,
   Familiar outskirts,
   Unboundaried fields,
   Along a country embankment
      That once carried trains
      We'd watched
      With wide-awed children's gaze.

Through cinder crunch and crosstie hollows,
      Last year's dead grass and rampant bramble,
      A lone bird's feather,
      Stray, rusted fishplates, spikes, dead flare caps —
Through all these, two lonely miles,
Rambled we that ghostly right of way
      To the trestle.

Skeletal and shorn of rail, road-bed and upper girder:
All that's left's the weathered
   Gracefully geometric bracework,
   Spanning faithfully, futilely
      Its familiar swampy abyss.
And, as when a child, I placed one foot
   Upon that despoiled threshold, (So did you).

Then tugged the wind at my chilled ear, and,
   Glancing down that narrowed steel lattice,
The child I was whispered gently, sadly:
   "No.
   It is safe, but you are not."
Strange, my friend: you did not see my thoughts,
   Nor hear that message teaching fear
      Where fear was not before.
      Down the approaching scarp we slipped;
My child-borne thought became a question:
Why, good friend, did you not hear?
Would you have crossed, unfearing, heedlessly,
      To the world we both left
      At that precipice?

NADINE D. MAJOR

MARCH, 1945

Do you remember when we were six and eight —
Or was it five and seven —
And lived in Camden during the war?
On Saturdays Gram would stay home and wash
On the old wringer maytag in the cellar,
Carrying the load up the stairs
To hang out in the yard, singing all the while
As we ran and played in the March fields
Running hatless through vacant lots
Like two kites in the cream-puff sky.

B.A. MANN

THE PLANTS

The Bushes all around were chattering —
Their tales were constant and unusual.
I decided never to give them my berries —
Mine were fresh when they weren't theirs.

And the clamor of the plants
sunk deep and quick in my moat,
Their songs could not survive my water;
My home was yet among the grass.

ONE LIFE SUMMER

A click of time progressed the hand;
My Mindglass sat, dripping sand —
A Thing was gone, a haze away
from touching fingers of Today.

I faded back, I caught the day;
one evening-summer we were Love,
A soft peachmildness felt your gifts.
Life came fast on large wheels speeding,
Life drove fast and fair one year
where that summer on the porch
Our blossoms swayed in moonlight sweetly.

117

THE WAVES OF LONELY

When high away she rode her flight
I muttered hate-oaths to the wall
(as I cast myself into the dejection
due her love), and to black and dank
Resource I fled my body and its passions.

The waves of stern and cruel Lonely lapped
against my bones.

THE FREEWAYS OF GOLD
(WHY I BECAME A HUNTER INSTEAD OF A COW)

Brown hands of Nicotine
Reach into my pocket,
onto my hand, into my mouth,
And crawl down my throat to feed.

Freeways of gold
Flashing in the sun
die in the dark
and shine the next day.
Diamond stripes on velvet arms
sit in the moonlight
awaiting the Resurrection.

Rows of cows with hemp-tied bridles
led me to a death-long trail
out of the Forest
    into the level ground.
Air with breathmarks gilded in gray
assumes my nose to need.

The Kings fix the horses
But occasionally lose to jockeys in sweaty underclothes
who are staked, their lives peasants.
They fixed me with their regal syllable
and tied my harness with cliches,
But I broke pace
    with an uncommon metaphor
and found a new Track.

I did it
    and they laughed.
    they laughed
And I laughed.

118

GAMBLER

Cigar stench, bitter drinks,
fast packups, hotel stinks,
forty hour table tops,
fifteen second toilet stops.

Shirts wilting on backs
and drooping in smell;
Three worthy pennies diced for, won;
Seldom daytimes, Indoor nights;
Breathing stale and thinking Survival.

These,
this ugly Set of possessions
Run me, crying,
down alleys into trashcans
until a possible Savior Collector.

BONNIE McCONNELL

THE TIGERS SO RENOUNCE THEIR NAME

One time we knew love wild and free from care —
a tiger and his tigress in their lair —
wherever we were close, love rampaged there.
One time love was feral with desire,
wanton with need, a laugh of purest fire,
world into world and all one world entire.

One time love was stallion-maned, and reared
on joyous hooves in music that we heard
more beautifully than that of any bird.
But what has happened to the joyous flame?
What broke the stallion, making him so tame?
And what made the tigers so renounce their name?

Now love — if this be love — is fierce no more.
Somehow, somehow, we stumbled through a door
that sealed love off from all it knew before .
I look at you and see a stranger. You
see strangers in my gaze (or say you do),
and neither one can say what makes this true.

I only know that all my touch has known
and loved, I must not touch. I know my own
flesh cringes with denial, to my bone.
It may be this is temporary — we
who've known too well, who've loved too well, may see
that love leap forth once more . . . God! let this be.

119

OBSESSED BY THE NEED

I am sick with my longing for
your brands like a poppied field
sown on me, lavish, as before!

I am faint with the need to yield
to your hands, to your intimate mouth,
to surrender to weapons you wield.

I am stricken by winds from the south
that speak of the nights caressed —
Now my body has known long drouth.

I am shaken by memories you pressed
over my heart . . . and obsessed
by the need of your hand on my breast.

AS NEAR LIKE AS CAN BE

I shall drink myself into a stupor —
or as near like as can be —
then let the rain fall, down all the dark
                    hours,
let it attack roof and tree;
let thunder, cataclysmic and blackened,
tromp its great boots on me.

Little I'll care for the wind's dark peril
or for the lightning's threat.
All through the wildness, I'll lie and giggle,
knowing they'll none of them get
any of me that has aught of importance —
and I? All that's gone, I'll forget!

INTO THE CREST

The sea breaks gold-green-white,
hard against the rocks,
and sundown's hazy light
nestles the air, the peaks,
kingly with foam, of sea —
Yearning for the deep
of emerald hush, in me,
untaken is the step

120

from air to caverns under
opal colored sky.
Reaching, inside me, wonder
beats to be set free.
Even my breath is fire
in this, my body's cell,
never to reach desire,
green with the sea's strange tale.
Mountaining waves are calling!
Into the white, cool crest,
now I must go, strength falling
even as I am lost!

ELLEN McCURDY

THE HARLEM GHETTO

See the slums of Harlem,
See children swarming the streets,
See the old men sitting on stoops,
I dare you; see unemployed standing on street corners.

In a driveway full of dusty dirt,
Stands an adolescent in disbelief,
And face downwards at the dirty door,
Stands a child in desolate depression.

Feel the yearning of youth in school,
Feel the frustration of young parents,
Feel the despair of wasted lives,
I dare you; feel the need to be human.

LYNNETTE McVEY

THE THINKERS

The dependent Swine
huddle together on

Formica
floors

      With Wood Paneling on all Sides
Formulating
   Ways
     to

Make life more
interesting or

Perhaps Worthwhile As they sift Through
Endless Papers that refer to a Revolution

in Mankind.
More wet

Minds Loom
ominously

Dripping with Formaldyhyde
As preserved with Time

Striving forward
for Something that

might offer Seclusion.

Ravaging the East and West. Garbage cans Obscure the
Quiet peace of Night.

Shaken forth, Bursting like Crimson
flowing in all Directions. Easter eggs

with Violent Men
Standing on top
Shaking fists as bearded Santas
With Pointed Ears Clasp their

heads in Nervous hands as they stand Shouting From
a Footstool That Shakes As Much As They Do.

DONNA MECKLER

Call loudly to the winds!
Ears have they none, nor care.
Their four-sided world is hollow
With their own billowing
And shallow echoing.

SUZANNE MARIE MEYER

WHEN DEW TURNS CRIMSON

When dew turns crimson from a dawn
that brushes the sea
like a golden mirror

122

And when eyes reflect the intensities
   of white-hot stars in a desert sky
   and warmth like snowing sunshine
Pours from crystal pitchers upon a land barren —
   sterile by the finiteness of man's mind —
     Making it luminescent
Then I will know where music has escaped to
   after it has been played
And we will dine on strawberries
   drink from honey-filled chalices
      And somewhere
      back in memory
      hidden
         by understanding and knowledge
A cock shall crow
and remember the blue sky that came before
     Night

MAN SHOULD DIE

Man should die
   his wars scrape the land like fire
burning the flesh of his own people
The poor starve
       while the rich argue over
              socialism
              capitalism
              communism
              man's rights
              poverty programs
Words that do not drop crumbs.
Infants scream for want of milk
   or something
     Something other than mud to fill their mouths.
Then there is green eyes
   and diamond teeth
dressed in a velvet jacket
   Eating caviar from pencil-thin fingers.
In fear man lives
   only to live
   another day
       in fear
         scorn
           mockery
             of his own blood.
Man should die.

RETURN

Claw
      Dissipate
incongruent spirit.
Till you lie crushed and bleeding
      asunder
and are nobody at all.
      Then
like a clock
tic in time
        normalcy the Ultimate.
andwecanfixyouwith
a grin
      like a Cheshire
        Cat.

MAUD I. MICHAELIS

THE DRAIN

The leaves from the tired trees blocked the drains
The road was a river; ankle-deep
    I stepped from the lawn into that swirling mass —
      and cleared the drain of leaves; —
  Above, I heard thunder
      but within me, the sound a shadow makes.

DAVID MOATS

BALLERINA

Flowing above as of liquid rhythm
Radiancy flaring
A lone ballerina
Absorbs a shuffling audience, and body singing,
Cries in the metamorphic delight of wine and tears.

The bows and reeds vibrate
And a wave of movement
Seeps forward to caress the toe of our
Graceful, graced living rhapsody:
A grape cries forth, a tear pours forth
And a deeply passionate vintage soothes a quivered lip.

124

The soaring arpeggio, our dancer,
Sings with an arm, a pirouette and a tear.
The tear is poured, offered, and magically
We cry at the richness of this, her wine.

No longer a woman,
Her form has changed from human to rhythmic
And her body breathes not
But leaps with the movement of song.
The orchestral catalyst taps her heart;
The grape is squeezed;
And music is made visible.

A sip of the grape
And her heart spins the eloquence of beauty;
A winesong flows
And her tears pour of rubious expression;
The fruit of her breast pounds us
And her purple song pervades our crystal night.

ROBERT MORGAN

THREE LOVES

through the trees of night
a shade of moonglow
touches us
ointment poured within us
and we are sleeping
crossed against the light
of a mere window

she whispered into me
je t'aime
softly then
beaucoup and
I marked her thigh
as a signal
of cruel love

the voluptuous star
between me
is her star
disappearing
into day

CRUCIFIXION OF THE IRON MAN

and she just swooped by
like a gazelle
held in captivity too long
all the way down she ran
from the skull of Golgotha
there hanging on a railroad tie
is the Iron Man
hopelessly alive
screaming to me from inside his casting
and begging for his molten state again
iron hung pure
as if to corrupt the shout of the sea
and make it laugh
with tears of melancholy
or corrode the shell of Proteus
so it sings sweetly
to the rhythm of old age
they are all here I believe
all the flies and ants and hornets
crawling away from these strange iron hands
like the Sabine women
indebted to Poussin and Rubens
torture is their beauty
solitude is horror
better to be alienated
than alone
guessing

THREE SIRENS

her face fell perfectly into meaning
found high in the darkness
of ubiquitous light
eyes cleaning their wings after flight
ready to go again if called by a lover
her star-line
was drawn in pursuit of a constellation
it followed the endless course of jade
her voice was my heart
in perpetual song
in her nakedness she held the olive branch
to eulogize the doves on a sunset strait

126

if she responds
with her eyes
smiling
when you ask
shall we die tonight
then she is a goddess

if I could see my own eyes
pouring their wonder into yours
then I would know our binding secret
and bury it forever

A MAN

a man only four feet high
lives in Chiusi
his domain is Etruscan art
pasta for breakfast and bees
from the Arno Valley
he loves the olive trees
the barren openness
his teeth are missing
and his trousers stink from sarcophagi
cats stalk the hillside there
and gather in black alcoves
wading the gutters to see him
he never kicks them aside as he should
for the cats in Chiusi
are xenophobic
and scratch redness
into the smart legs of archeologists
this man is a curator of crypts
dishes and tombs
eyebrow sticks and misery potions
the art he sees in yesterday
is cruel work
the life of thousands
driven by the night noise
the drone of feline idiocy

127

A LESSON

for breakfast
I had the following: five medium
slices of bacon with
two fried eggs
(I ate these first
because a decent man is not
permitted to let them
cool down)
then I drank
a glass
of jus d'orange with a yellow
and green pill   my coffee
I drank persistently
sipping at first until I was sure
it would not scorch
the mouth
responsible for
intake

DONALD JAY MOSES

I was bicycle riding along alone Montauk Highway and I saw this
guy walking along the road and I stopped to ask him how far it was
to Amagansett. He said "Oh it's pretty far you know . . . about
four miles." I said I do not care about its looks but thank you for
the information.
I peddled on.
Man, that guy was wrong. It was not that far at all.

I was biking along alone Montauk Hgy and I saw this guy in a car
and I stopped to ask him how far it was to Amagansett, and he
said "It's just a couple of miles down the road." I thanked him
for the information .
I peddled on.
Boy, that guy was wrong, it was a hell of a ride, all the way on
an uphill grade.

i was biking along alone montauk hgy and i saw a guy at an air-
field in an airplane, & i stopped to ask him how far to Am'g'ns'tt.
he said "you're practically there already." i said thanks,
& peddled on.
needless to say, he was so wrong he must have been out of his mind.

i was bombing alone m'nt'k hwy in my jet powered car & f'r laugh
i ask'd s'me guys walk'g & driv' & fly'g h'w f'r to 'm'g'ns't. boy
(man) wh't a g's, i n'ver ev'n he'rd th'r 'nsw'rs, 'cause i p'st th'r
b' for th'y c'ld sp'k.

128

HAMID NAFICY

SUMMER, '66

the woman
looked down
from high above; looked parallel to the lines of her eyes.
in front of her she found her child, who
was melting away and dying away from the shining of the sun.
she contemplated that this child had
incarnated her past;
with trees growing out of his body in the green space.

and, now, this man was truly her existence who
was swung to her by the balance of time.

here, i am the bitterfleshed gazelle
whose chanting is the Molavi's flute, and the meadows,
lone observers of my forlornness.

the woman looked away from him. drew in
her look with bitterness. and a smile
begun gardening in her face. she
started talking: of me, of all that i have been and she has been.
the Molavi's flute was weeping. and i was ear, and chanting was
climbing up in me smokelike.
i stopped in myself. suddenly.
like a carriage
whose horse is frozen into a statue of ice.

but, a violent explosion
splattered my head to the space. and my body, headless,
with its blue blood, continued its way
without turning back and looking at her.

like remorseful chickens
the lines of her look returned to their eggs,
and the horizon admitted her child to himself.

3-8-'66

a door opens
a door closes,
and the word remains silent
between that opening and closing.

i comprehend the power of being
and the egg that day after day
grows in us
ceaslessly.

129

Being is an endless integrity. but
the nights here are heavy
and the yeast of my words pregnant.

doors open
doors closed
and a word in between —
silence

and the solitude that relates
you and i to others.

EVE NORTON

THE SALTIMBANQUES (PICASSO)

Hard-edged
under the tree (among the tiny stones)
sleep the saltimbanques
dead-seeming.

Let her breath
blanket
and mingle with his black dreams
in warm ascending stream.

Let her mouth plant a plus on sufficient bliss
never owning direction
random wire leap splits
for fine high wires
        brushing.

                    Cut of shanks
              crossing
              in larger diamonds
                    Hard edges of black
              crossing
               pink.

              Nose to nose
              the saltimbanques sleep
              loosely
              Their dreams ascending rings
Tall,   of diamonds
    free,   black
invented for   on pink.
the upstretched
arms of love.

Tumbling lone
silent
on the grasses (among the
hills and trees and pebbles).

130

Flingers
of laughing
babychildren, reverse head-
standers,
hand-walkers,
        all this . . .
and the sadness of sleeping:

The saltimbanques
    are snow crystals
Angles
    melting into
    the curves of time.

CHARLES OEHMCKE

SELF

Bones, soul, sack of man,
Midway bend in yon corner
Where mill's wall
Meets mill's floor.
Or uncomposed lie,
Floppy, atop the pile,
Or crushed beneath,
Or stand stiffly pressed,
Dizzily leaning with the crowd.
Or freely fall, splitting and ripping,
Pouring forth through jagged tear
Upon the fertile soil
Whence you yourself made yourself.
Now, your vital contents spring to life,
Perpetual, eternal life.

BILL F. OLIVE

PRETTY CYCLE

A mushroom grows
beneath the lavatory
where wood oozes
good things
        Or a clever
brown spongy
strong fungus
has a sprout of
definite shape
spring forth
perfect a day
and blacken
and fall in two
and on its right
The Thinker
figures the mushroom
has to be there later

131

IF BILLY IS GOING TO BE NICE

      For her I had passion
deeply see.
      Was how I went for her
went with seasons changing
wept my seasons brought.

      Turn of a year I lost my dog
putting it off in
a blind part of me
for were
chances to be bought
and I believed I had her.
      Hurt me
blindly I dreamed of my hound.

      Well you see he
was the best dog
in the world
      and she the best girl.

      Well ma'm
but when you lose your beagle hound.
      Was a season.
      Even if
you're mad at your animal
and love your bitch.

      It is even though
a cause for sanity.
      A thing
so hard to take
when you don't have it here.
      Don't have it and
sanity is too heavy
madness too hungry.

      See madness needs
more nourishment
blood
      soul.

      And live on moving
quitting fooling.
      Reach a treasure.
      Luck had it thanks.
      This one she is.
      Women are
the realistic medicine I've learned.

MICHAEL OLSON

A QUIET COLD

It is a quiet cold tonight.
The quiet cold of the centuries.
The stars laugh as I ponder their mystery,
A quiet cold laugh of secret knowledge.

ELLEN M. O'NEILL

I DREAM OF YOU STILL

I dream of you still, of the happier days,
Of frost-bitten winters, and clover-drenched Mays.
I still hear your laughter, so distant it seems,
Coming back on the wings of our half-forgot dreams.

How strange and how sad that these treasures so rare,
We let slip through our fingers with never a care.
And now you are gone, and my loneliness wells,
In the smothering darkness where memory dwells.

Too swiftly the days of our youth melt away,
Like dewdrops caught up in the sun's golden rays.
Dissolving in memories of smiles and of tears,
Only to beckon us down the long years.

LARRY OWEN

A WILTED ROSE

O, My Luve is like a wilted rose,
That's dried with a gentle hue.
O, my luve is like the rhapsody,
The rhapsody played in blue.

As dismal thou art my creepy lass,
So stupidly in luve am I,
And I will fake it longer still my dear,
Till the coke machines gang dry.

Till the coke machines gang dry my dear,
And the corn flakes wi' the sun!
And I will snow thee still my dear,
While the wheels of time shall run.

As fair as a bell my only luve,
And fair as a bell awhile!
And again I will come my luve,
Though it will be a long, long while.

Out I strolled one day, and caught the tail of a
    Rainbow.
Upon the red I climbed holding to the blue and
    Yellow.
The bright sun shown and radiated my way until the
    Tail melted.
Down I looked and saw the brook smile and the mountains
    Tear shed.
Laugh Hubert, glow and wink stars of the psyche
    Illuminated.
To the top I climbed and hurdled over sour light to
    The moon.
I landed on compassion and forgiveness and stared
    And gaped at entity till noon.
I smoothed peanut butter rumination onto intellectual
    Bread,
I ate. Then I smiled, cleaned the knife with my heart
    And decided to stay.

ROBERT PARSONS

HER

I

Walk through our Summer's garden
To where the roses flow
Over and around a sheltered arbor
That whispers of another time.

II

Walk with me to our roses
Their petals now awhite
Their veins apale like frost
Upon a withered flower.

Sit in our sheltered arbor
Of wood and vine turned pallid
And long lengths of frigid glass
Flowing coldly from above.

III

All Sterile sterile white
That which bloomed so well,
Only memory of Summer's blossoms
That never stood the cold.

MAKE IT PURE-BRIGHT

To hell with the chalky world
Of shallow men with shallow feelings.

If I must be anguished
Make it pure-bright jagged pain.
But if I capture joy
Let it true and brilliant be.

I want to be no madman
Nor wildly arrayed.
I want only real feelings
Of living vivid colors.

WAITING TO BE BORN

Ten minutes, ten minutes I walk with her a
week –- talking little talks by unseen rules that mean I may
not love her. But I do.

On my love I must be silent. I can talk
about apple cores or friday nights; but about my love I
must be silent. For if I told her my soul could not abide the
rules she would say it could not be, must not be, will not be,
and vanish.

For she doesn't love me. Her eyes no longer
twinkle, her lips will not kiss me back. And yet she is all
there really is for me.

I still persist in hope. Not because there is
hope but because I cannot do otherwise. She is ever present,
always there and bursting into presence whenever I pause a
moment.

I am little pieces all assembled waiting for
her to breathe me life. For I am not really anything worth
anything without her love. I am a form all hollow without a
soul.

I must wait patiently for her love to give me
life with a breaking, bursting, impatient love. And I fear I will
never be no matter what I do . . .

JOHN PEAK

SEPTEMBER

And the angels having
Switched on their lights
Raised their shades
And caused a distant, scattered
Brilliance in the night.

And pricked again the pitch of sky
With their own added gleam
Of frustrated jealousy, it seemed
Of an isolated, sleepy luster
And vainly again they might try
To draw from an intensity transfixed
Flowing from eye to eye.

AND THEN YOU WOKE IN THE DARK

And a curtain rises slowly
On an empty house
And you can hear it behind you
And feel the absence of sound.

And blackened bricks are framing a
Flickering red and yellow city
That shifts its weight, praising itself
With red streamers that wave
As they rush upward in a tangled crowd.
And the island of light heats
Your half-closed eyes and hers
so you can only feel her quietly
Worshiping body against yours.

And your sealed eyes see her
wrapping around and around
Flowing, continuous rhythm
Drowns the animal sound
Pressing on your face —
And throat-flesh pulsing; closing
Closing, beating, crushing-wet,
Hot, slipping, yielding force
Clinches and suffocates you

And then you woke in the dark
And you heard the curtain behind you
And felt again the numbing absence of sound.

136

THE MEMORY

And he spoke again,
"How is it that you
Can be so afraid of me?
Being dead, I naturally couldn't
Hurt you — if she
Wanted me to.
But she doesn't.
Is it because screws,
And dirt
And three months, not to mention
Several
      Kinds
          of shrouds
Couldn't keep me under?''

And he winked,
And sat down, lighting a cigarette,
And laughed an ugly laugh.

FROM KNOWING INFIDELITY

Detachedly eyeing his severed hand
He shoves the spurting stump in his pocket
Trying to hide the disgusting
Portrayal of his injury
From smirking eyes that yet
See a spreading spot of wet cotton
With unfeigned indifference.

Shrimp-boat light, a luminescent lizard eye
On an oiled marble desert
Indiscernably blended with a finely blemished
Tar-paper dome
And a pier-post stool
And behind — a highway — empty for
Over a year.

LYLE PEAKE

THE INNER JUNGLE

How could I, in truth
Ever say my soul is silent?
It is the beat of drums
At night.
Throbbing for an unknowing

137

Cause.
What am I? A fool? A Mortal?
Too short of life on earth.
If lived how could I repay
Those endless lessons
Once taught?
Could I hope to gain
An understanding
Of what is?
I am I.
That is all I know.
A million I's
Swarming in search
Endlessly
For Awareness
A search for Self Truth.
The I's have it.
I am I.
Nothing more need I be.
No chain can drag my soul
Into oblivion.
As I
I am Infinite
I shall be forever
Not here
Not there
But in Eternity.

WILLIAM H. PERRY

URBAN PERPLEXITY

Massed concrete, steel and wood,
Smoke ascending, a darkening hood;
Flamboyant forms spaciously embracing;
Irregular dimness, widespread placing.

Structures varied, old and new;
Myriad patterns bold in view.
Densely wed industry, ugly relation;
Subsistence for existence; meager elation.

Dawn emits the populace, a human rain.
Intermittant travel in faltered strain.
Innumerable ways mid push and daze;
Relentless motive in obscure haze.

NO SECRETS URSULA

No secrets Ursula, nothing to find out,
Only a simple, murmuring shout.
No words to say; gloomy and dark is my way
Where worries hurt and slowly slay.
No secrets Ursula; now everything is known.
True it is I've never grown
Into a man for my life has shown
Only a rebel drifting into another
Sad and lonely fix as the clock slowly ticks.
Always the same wandering and dreaming and
Wondering and trying to understand.
I never kept a plan; down some back street I ran.
Always lost in a dim retreat,
Where sorrow and pain ever meet.
To search for beauty I'm inclined,
But the turning heart has no mind.
No secrets Ursula; now all is known:
To flaying winds this life is sown.

NOAH PESSAH

HOW TO PERSIST?

What for the lyric warble
About the fractured marble
In our dim, passing day
Of a moony, yearning way,
During our short, restless life
That mostly cuts like a knife
And everyday newspage
Shivers from Atomic Age?

Certainly, the axiom is not new
That existence is a hard clue,
Unmovable by sheer flattery,
Plays out like a motionless battery,
Dispossessed of vital thread,
Falls into the darkness of death.
Thus all endeavors are in vain
As none will see us again.
But that's the soothing gain,
Gained in acute, hellish pain!

139

Listen, something from afar
Like a Russian samovar
Huskily, tiredly dreams, screams an ancient bell
For religious service: Hu, ha, too much pollution
In your well! Hu, ha, too much hell
In this dolorous, sinful, tearful dell!
How to exist? How to persist?
In this unendurable mist?

Keep imagination on duty about a lady.
Heaven forbid! Not a Delilah,
Not a Jezebel, not a Xanthippe!
But a dame of noble character,
Of blessed distinction
And of relative beauty.
Then wait unremittingly
For the desired marvel
To fix the fractured marble! . . .

MY WINE

I reached another birthday.
Humility is in process.
Sterility is in progress.
Fertility is in regress.
Immunity, come by express!
Still sounds like counting.
But it does not eye
Any more like mounting
As the years roll by —

I travel further through a fractured globe,
A tortured planet, a twisted world and
A stormy life splashed with cloudy years.
I travel further in a cracked vehicle,
On a crooked road, in dull weather,
As God is my driver
And He drives me
Warily —

Once in a while
I read hot things
— Where simple laws
Of nature are set
Down in words
Of beauty —
To make my old,
Rusty soul go young —

This time — about
A bride without
A wedding dress,
A garden path,
A florist box
And a fig leaf —

Just this is my champagne.
Just this is my pine.
Just this is my wine.

JULIE PHILLIPS

REALITY

Blazing headlights light
   the slim, white ribbon of highway,
Peering out the car window
It seems as if the entire world
Abruptly stops at the end of the lights;
The blackness of night
   encloses everything beyond,
All that is left is
   the small patch of light in between,
And it is not real,
Neither is the nothingness ahead.

TRAGEDY

A jet-black automobile slinks through busy thoroughfares,
Making its way to a quiet, deserted acre.
Abruptly it stops amid sugar maples sighing in anguish;
Eight youths somberly remove the slim, gray metal box,
Their gloved white hands smooth the red, white, and blue cloth;
Mute with grief, they march silently past downcast faces
Whose presence is the public tribute;
Questions, deeply felt, but until now unspoken
   come rushing from friends —
"He's dead — and for what . . . why did this have to happen?"
Once again, the demands of a far-off war have come home.
The death of our young men is freedom's tragic price.

VICTORS

Their lips melted,
Their warm bodies were one,
Her arms would not release him,
His fingers gently held her face;
Outside the world was black,
Inside they were alive,
Victors of the night.

BELIEF

There is no Santa Claus
Says the wicked —
No tooth fairy,
No Easter Bunny,
No Peter Pan;
There is no world of make-believe.

How cruel to say that
There is no far-away land of lolli-pops;
It is to take the glow from a child's face,
To destroy his dreams.

For to be a child is to be something
    very different from the man of today;
It is to believe in love,
To believe in loveliness,
To believe in belief;
It is to be so little
That the elves can reach to whisper in your ear,
It is to turn pumpkins into coaches,
Lowness into loftiness,
And nothing into everything.

There is no cause to disillusion youth,
No need to open their eyes,
Time and youth will pass all too soon;
Let them believe while they can.

DAVID W. PINCHBECK

THE PRIEST

He stands with bread on his left hand,
Wine on his right,
And people at his feet,
But there is dirt on his hands.

142

MARCUS H. PINI

THE PARTY

the night bends
in hungry grief . . .
closed for the day
they are suspended around —
seeking each other
in stable holdings . . .
anxiously stroking
each other's arms,
       circle
       rise — fall
       circle . . .
striping the tops
of their fingers.
       circle
       rise — fall
       circle . . .
           circle circle
             fall . . .

and out their mouths
flowing forgotten tears.
in their zealous searches,
narrow cats . . .
they find always
only a mirror.

and are kissing
by coming and going
       stroke . . .
touching to feel to be close in,
       fingering . . .

a glasseye revels
in almondcolored remembering.
well preserved pillow
beside a strong
man's sleep.

143

LONELY WORLD

gluttering woman
   — alone
walks with a secretive smile
keeps a hidden cage . . .
feathered world
amid sliding stone massives,
     a trembling hand
speaks with the scared
fledgling body.

softer
   softer
      and softer
      his peeps
      are disappearing.

MARGIN NOTES

sleepwalking days
     and
       intermediate . . .
steps turning around
     twisting —
parchment of autumn
fleeing burning flakes.
as mute transience
far in the woven
background the marks
of a broken window.

the luxury of time
     is consuming . . .
Margin Notes up
in the dense air —
finally the tune
     has arrived.

word of her was very near,
     lurking
     waiting
close to my ear —
losing weight
becoming bodiless . . .

faces drifting around me
     fragmented . . .
     Margin Notes.

SANDY LYNN POSLEY

THAT BRING MALIGNANT RAINS
(For Richard G. Watts)

A sky falls softly, like the beaded rays
Of sun that deftly fill a bladed weed,
Calls softly into grass and brittle hays
To wonder-dampened hills and flutist's reed.
Like midnight catching twitching cricket sound,
Like daytime catching dark, flirtatious night,
Like subtle vines that quickly spread and bound,
To tie the waiting ground and guileless light,
A pain creeps soft. Not knowing lonely tears
You do not try to stop, but let it be.
And listen, then, with eyes and childish ears,
That hear and look and feel but do not see.
      A sky falls softly dropping danger chains
      Of silent drops that bring malignant rains.

OF WHAT I AM

Midnight fog like morning dampness
Curls around my waist and
Mimics the form that is only a
Pretense of what I am.
Coldly, it caresses my hands
And my cheeks,
Catches the sound of
Drifting trains,
Entwines the lonely whisper of
Loving absent hands and distant chains,
Returns the glance of empty streets,
Uncaring, smiles and passes by.
Intensity and silence
Awake the empty sea and charge
The lifeless wind that seeks to
Hold it back, the holdless terror-scream
Of night that kills in loneliness
The shallow fool
Who mimics unperceptive past and fog.

145

PRECIOUS STONE

Light-shattered space peeking in at my window
Eyes blinking innocently,
Watching, curious,
Strange man on earth that is not so strange,
Sugar-peppered darkness and void
Gently touching, catching, holding bits of
    precious stone.
Warm stone,
Earth, a pulsing pebble,
Sparkles of light which do not search, but find.
A man lost among the trees looking . . . for a single
    poppy seed.
And heavens splashing, calling, saying:
Here. Everywhere. All.

BILLIE CAROL POWELL

WHY?

Undying love makes for the destruction of a soul.
It is the most sorrowful, yet challenging sacrifice ever to be
seen. The crowd outside awaits silently yet eagerly for the
approaching ceremony.
Time races in the heat of passion, lovers rarely listening for
the ticking of a clock or for the sounding of a gong.
Words come slowly as lips search hungrily for the fulfilment
of lust and desire.
Hand in hand they walk down the sun bathed lane,
Leaving the glowing warmth to venture into the cool, green
mossy world of the forest, where only the splashing sound of
a trinkling stream as its races through its shallow bed
to the lake disturbs the silence.
And now the lovers speak not, but listen to the rhythm of
the other's beating heart.

The fading sun begins its descent.
The two emerge, shaded in shadows of gold,
They part, one going eastward to await the reincarnation
of day, the other facing the westward sky.
Amidst the beauty of the falling shadows the last fading
strands of sunlight descend upon a tear drenched face.

Time has passed.
Spring has reached the peak of its expression,
Summer has soothed and prolonged the memories of the
relationship and summoned forth new means of expressing love,
But as winter winds whip through the trails they climbed,
as drifts of snow cover their green fields of happiness,
She walks away - - - -
Away from the loneliness and the tears —
Away to the fulfilment of a dream where lips spouting forth
the sweet nectar of love can never disturb the cold stillness
of her heart.

JOHN MICHAEL PRESCOTT III.

SPRING

I lie on cool grass

the sky is clear
a bird calls
     and
the wind fans me . . . with . . . timed . . . breaths
a tree shades my head

I hope no one comes near

EXPERIENCE

As I sit here ripe in ponder
Thoughts arise and memories wander.
Reckoning times of yesteryear,
Deeds envisioned without fear;

My love's now dormant beneath the soil;

Summer is fading, winter's coming,
Shadows deepen, memory's running.
Candles flicker, time drips by,
Youthful yearnings soon will die.

LARRY PRICE

Love and I walked the black river
With winged feet, we dreamed of crossing
Into happiness and purity.
We thought, so much is good.

A small stream joined the river.
Light blue water
Ran over the remnants of Magdalene's stoning.
Enchanting.

In its celebrating
We melted to one.
Willing by both,
A gentle lyric act —

I wept over love.
Quickly; unplanned words and thoughts
(was I myself not a foundling left from a foundling?)
More quickly came finality
Unbeckoned; dreaded and desired —

And then love left
To bathe in the river.
Entranced, I saw a warm body
To fill any emptiness.
A breeder of sons
Who would be wont to taste the likes of their Mother.
I watched as she washed away
The essence of myself that clung to her.
I wondered the stars

I was struck!

That glorious magnificent yellow star
Sent a bolt through my heart
That slew every precedent.
Keeper of souls,
I must have that star.

Love raises her head.
The features come as cold and angular
As a machine slut.

Bitch!

148

Wade with stone in hand,
Smile — slowly
Strike

Skull of myself cracks
Eyes weep blood
Twice more I strike
And then I am dead.

JAMES PRIDGEON

A SEMI-POEM DEDICATED TO GAIL

In this place of changing forms;
    Or should I say time for place.
In this indecisive moment and all others till that
Day — that time of Fullness . . .

    The clouds here will roll over the tops of
Mountains; beyond the temporal hills, timeless
Clouds will roll and promise rain for the road
Nearer than the hills —
    Will promise rain for the roofs and
The concrete below the dusty window, over the
Autumn leaves, fallen.
    A day for Rain;
        Promised by all those timeless travelers,
    across the Dust,
        Promised the Rusting house tops
        And the Blind Grayness, with
        Autumn resting on the surface — waiting to give sight
        Through the spotted half reflector.

    So much more to yield, save darkness
    As they roll too high.

THERE IS NO TIME THAT ABOVE THIS — HOPE

        Oh the ragged eagle soars
        Above the sands
        And weeping shores.

        And what does one know,
        And what can one care
        That I have done this?

Time?

There is no time to listen for
A heartbeat in the cities
   Or feel the notes of forlorn ditties.

There is no time to watch the
Flickering of the lamps
   Or hear the sighs of hollow tramps.

There is no time for men to learn of
Nothing.

E. M. PRISE

COMPRENDRE C'EST PARDONNER

A small shadow on the wall,
A large struggling soul

The first glimpse into the comprehending
Shy blue lights reveals

If you're one of the "in" souls
Who *know* . . .

Know the noble torment of duty
When care has flown

And a philosophic resignation
While driving "home"

As the deep abyss of escape
Fills with vague, fleeting justifications!

Is this Life?

ELEANOR PUSATERI

WHILE WE WAIT

whispered words weaving silent sounds
while mindless men make mockery of death,
painful grunts grow weaker as gruntless pains grow greater
while curtain-cut complaint compounds complaint.

heartless heroes having hardships
while heavy hearts hear only helping heels,
merciless mountain makers making mountains
while clammy hand clasps kleenexed clammy hand.

the breath of death blows bright the breath of Life
while sunday sinner's breath breathes smokeless,
weary women weeping futile tears
while wiseless wisemen thank stars and lesser lights.

S. R. RAMES

POEM

whisper to me
as if I were the night
and you didn't want the crickets
to overhear

be the wind
for a moment please
and rustle the leaves
inside me

but here comes daybreak
look out babe
I'm flyin' away

TWO POEMS OF A DIFFERENT COLOR I THINK

I

mod Now
dipshit
'scuse my French
gotta spit
makes me sick
all of it

you too
thirty-eight

II

I hereby apologize
for that first poem

151

NARASIMHIAH RAMESH

WHERE?

Whence I came
I know not,
Whither I go?
I know not.
Now whence
All darkness
before and after.
A patch of work
Here an island,
Some respite.
Childish laughter ringing
Far behind
Aging wails
Far in front.
My thoughts I
Close to these.
But the rising
swell of time
Is fierce and
growing fast.
Alas this island is
shrinking smaller.
This patch of work
This respite
is over.

EDWARD C. RAMIREZ

ONE-ONE

One plus one
Add eternity.
One less one —
Nonentity.

LILAC

Lilac tree in purple bloom
By the window of my room.
Dew in leaves,
Enchantment near,
And the lilac, sweet and clear.

152

I ENVISION BEAUTY THERE

I see rainbows blending high,
Stretching far across the sky.
I see buds appear around
In the cool, wet, dewy ground.
I envision beauty there
Where the earth lies cold and bare.

THE DEPTH OF LIVING

My cheeks are dry over your grave
Though my heart is wet with grief.
You leave a life of noise and emptiness
for a silent bed below.
You take a soul to ponder its decaying flesh.
The depth of living becomes the depth of dying.
The wonder of a man pales into oblivion,
Yet, only the sod remembers and awaits him.
No more the puff of human breath against the seasons,
No more the sound of human troddings upon the avenues
of earthly gain and failure.
The world shuts out the voice of man to tend to
Its own echo and vanity.
The world knows no human sorrow,
For man is brief,
Small,
And unfamiliar — only I remember you.
I am human too.

EGRAM RAMS

CIVILIZATION

The dove fell from his perch;
He's lying on the ground.
Blood red blood oozing.
His white feathers soiled;
From the mud and muck.
Sports cars, trucks, and taxis
Hurrying to get nowhere.
Making tread marks
Back and forth over his whiteness.
Unheeding, uncaring, grinning.
Always grinning enigmatic.

153

Smile, smile at pain;
At destruction, at agony;
Disfigured, smile, poverty, smile,
Fire, flood, war, death,
Smile, smile, always smile.
Suffer, suffer, make them happy.
Suffer little childrenlike
The pure white dove.
Changing, ever changing
Hurry, hurry, ever hurrying
To go where? To meet what?
New, newer, better, more.
Never enough of anything.
New today, obsolete tomorrow
Bigger, always bigger, bigger.
Big house, big car, much bigger.
Buildings, machines, bombs!
Especially bombs, huge, huge!
Cause suffering for more and more.
Bigger wars, faster death;
Always faster, faster, faster.
Quick, quick, get there first.
Push the little things out,
Out of your hurrying way.
Get there first, better, faster.
You're there first, better, faster.
Where to now? For what?
More hurrying, still faster.
First, first, always first.
Fly faster than the wind,
The sound, faster than light.
Then still hurry, hurry some more.
Hurry to die, cause death,
Unnoticed, never look at death.
Kill, kill and keep going faster.
Never notice the white dove;
Now ground into the earth.
Part of the ground, dust particles.
Blending, unnoticed, back again,
To the beginning, the start,
From where he came.
Never to return? Dead, gone?
Does anyone care? Even notice?
Why did he fall to the ground?
Become bruised, mangled, dirty?
The false smile? The speed?
Speeding to destruction?

154

Lust for the big, the better?
The fastest? Quicker deaths?
What killed *Him?* Time?
Man? Civilization? Civilized,
Thats what the world is,
Civilized. Be civilized, kill,
Destroy, better, bigger, faster.
The small white dove of peace
Died, quick, fast, civilized.
Damn civilization!!!!!!!!!

ENID HESTER RHODES

SONETTO SENZA RIMA

When all the laughter and the tears we shared
Have shattered with the brittleness of glass
And nothing in my eyes remains except
The scattered fragments of that once so bright
And precious unreality, that once
So mystic melody beyond the music
You composed and chanted me (the splintered
Remnants now have faded from my eyes),

I pause to stare, and seeing clear, as if
I looked before me through a fishbowl at
The turbid, turgid waters of our short
Uneven past, I stop and counterfeit
A laugh at you and at myself, a voiceless
Laugh like yours, as empty as your love.

KEN RICCI

HAIKU

I long to bite the
Full white moon; have its juice run
Down around my chin.

Two nuns, white veiled on
A noon splashed rock. The waves play
With their blowing skirts.

Across the darkened
Pond a ripple spreads, wrinkling
The moon's reflection.

155

DAVE RICH

TO GAIL

Your hair speaks of the first beginnings of things,
While your lips proclaim the fullness of summer.
Your voice is strangely filled with winter,
But your smile partakes of all seasons.
When our hands first met did you also hear
The far-off cry of wild birds?

PSALM 151

Enough of this postponing!

This moment I shall begin to live the life I was
    born for.

I shall walk out into the moonlight and stand there
    for hours and hours.

(Oh, I shall know what it is that sets the wolves to
    howling.)

And I shall lie down in public places in broad daylight
    and close my eyes.

(Who knows? Perhaps I wish to practice the art of
    dying.)

 Yes! And I shall revisit the shores of my childhood
    and listen to what the waves are saying to the sand.

(The same old secret, but always so welcome.)

And I shall let the hills of desire caress my eyes
    at last.

(The tree-covered hills, the fern-covered hills.)

Yes! And I shall stand on the brink of day and
    witness the birth of light.

That's where I'll be . . . at the brink of day.

Look for me . . . look for me there.

156

RELIEF AT BIG BASIN

The redwoods seem unaware it is Monday
And I am still not working.
They whisper and sigh to me so ardently,
I am almost embarrassed.
I think I shall sit down
Under this tree beside the path
And contemplate the mystery of leaves.
Perhaps I shall be discovered at last
By the tribe I have sought so desperately:
That gentle tribe,
That tribe which will not require me to kill
    my brothers and sisters.
The ferns tell me it is so.
I shall wait
Here . . . under this tree
Beside the path.

BONNIE L. RIEDERS

ARTESIAN

parched
red
corpuscles
grasping
downward
in contiguous
caring
circles
to the
essence
where the
heat
of existence
melts
and a
soft
screaming
voice is
heard
through the
cool
neverending
cool blue
liquid

157

TERRESTRIAL

a cloud is killed by a stone
and its death is soon forgotten
yet ants continue to rape trees

leaves are hurting stones
yet trees still regress
to heckle the moon
as do storms
who conspire
with the weeds
to torture every ant

the sky is wounded by a branch
and it curses all birds
as petals are being
frightened
by lusty bees
and gnarled roots
detest
the stars at dawn

craving
the hallowed warmth
which scorns
the cold
most flowers
wilt

but somewhere
yes
somewhere
strong sun
still caresses
soft blue waters

LUCIA MORSE RIMBACH

WHERE IS THE GLORY?

Today we walk in darkness,
With darkness stifled scream.
Lament, O Gods of Wisdom!
Among men there is no dream.

Their souls are warped with hate,
Their brains are bullet bound;
Their flesh is but a target
For violence to ground.

Scum of lust and evil
Is military might,
Ah, Strumpets of the jungle
Parade your armor bright.

Must man dress up to kill?
Is it the Nations' will?
Damon and Pythias, both are dead.
War is a harlot, whom men have wed.

BRUCE ESTES RIPPETEAU

In tears and tinsel
She knelt down and kneeling cut the green soft
Stem of a Chrysanthemum
Deep running fish in a calm ocean while a world war
Raged above tin fish occasionally
Peter who followed is walking
In the desert and every other step he walks in the
Artic like alternating bands or flickering worlds
    So hot and panting and noisy and sticky
With the medics and some of my buddies each
With his carbine huddling over my dirty camouflage
I was so grateful for someone waving a bandage
To cool my burning face
The green sap flowed into my mouth and I could
                          not breathe
Eyes closed
Eyes open
Watching the blast come out and kiss away
                    the flesh
Same slowness as cold air   cascading
Off a letter saying he was
Grenaded in a firefight   that he will
Give life to no more flowers
      And you have
Cut the last of them

159

. . . the trellis in the Fall
   the minutes the red sun shimmers in the cooling
        evening over the highway past a
        housing project
   a wet rose in the garden
   the tame stars circling the eves
   snowfall
   snowmelt
   the greenness growing
   April twigs over the gardener's sundial
   a patch-wet concrete apron drying in sunny
        snow day as 707's hurry past on
        a February runway . . .

THE WATER THAT BLOOMED THE CRAB APPLE DROWNED MY TURTLE

Today was rainy and miserable
and I buried my turtle who
died last night found him floating around
but never raising his head and that was five-thirty
I got a dish and put medicine in it
and water and propped my dead pet turtle
up so he could breathe and be warm by
the light at six. Today was rainy and
its the kind flowers like I think for even
the backyard tree broke its buds festooned
pink with the life bearing water that misted
about last night and today was a
wet shoe day at three. My turtle was resting
on the pebble in the water as before but not
really looking at anything and so at four
I rinsed him off went into the rain
spooned out a hole by the pink tree four inches down
and faced him west. Cut and pulled out
healthy roots and softened his bed, packed
the dirt leaving my dead pet turtle beneath
the water again

I meant to put a flower seed there so when
the pure petals drank the mist I'd know whose
guts the roots pierced. I meant
to think a goodbye thought but stepping
on the compacting dirt roof of which all
is engendered and all of a love returned I can
not help but add at twelve midnight a pitcher
of water for the long dry day tomorrow.

160

SHIRLEY D. ROBINSON

FAMILY

Horse:
Alive,
Brisk,
Trotting on.
Flowing mane.
Plume of tail.

Mare:
Gravid,
Worn,
Dozing now.
Drooping eye,
Listless, sad.

Foal:
Tiny,
Graceful,
Gay of soul.
Sucking Life
From wasted shell.

LAURA ROTHMAN

THAT PERSON

Someone I loved very much died
How dead, I'm not sure
But I can't help wishing and hoping That Person would come
      back to life
The only trouble is . . . now I'm not certain That Person was
      alive in the first place
Perhaps I take my dreams too seriously.

LOUIS HENRI ROUSSO

DEATH'S DREAM KINGDOM

And Birth and copulation and death.
Mankind has looked life in the eye and spat
The spittle of a deaf, dumb, and blind man.

I have been born and had it once,
Then had it again;
And now I wait for the fragments of life to be collected.

That glorious day when the falling rain
Will collect in a stream that flows, but does not move,
Down the sewer to Death's Dream Kingdom.

161

MARILYN RYE

NOW

The mud is mixed from blood, not water.
The land yields a rich harvest of nothing.
Fields are seeded with bodies of children.
The wind passing through their mothers' bones
Croons softly thinking that they sleep.
Rivers are dammed by the flesh of their fathers.
And those that live have forgotten how to weep.

BARBARA ELLEN SALERNO

I

Did you ever see a do-do bird
Embalmed in ancient dust
Perhaps he's contemplating
The worthlessness of us

II

ah victim of acquaintance daily
whence come you accoutred so gaily
your elegance is culture's peak
what business with me do you seek
if placed upon a scale were we
your social grace would outweigh me
but yet in worth the scepter i hold
above that decadence —
                              your soul

W. H. SCHAEFER
Translated by Ruth Bonura

EULOGY

Fate this?
Lightning out of a clear, blue sky kills
spring's child, plugging anemone and clover
sitting in the early morning's dewy grass.

162

A joke of heaven, which — because we are looking
close to that ground meant only for the lowly worms
and worry, worry —
wants us to know,
like laughter from the seats of gods
what we are able to.

Nodding in the south wind the blue bell,
insects ring it gently,
sleeping-thin spiders shimmering labor.
Up, up.

Summer's linen, sinking back into the crumb of soil
teaches us one thing and
makes us wonder:
how, and how blessed, does one live that long?

GOD EVERGREEN

Century, you, why must you be called the damned one?
Blackened by burns, the temple is accusing: God is dead.
The king decays, no longer good enough for even such as mice.
Butcher is emperor. And bloody rules his red.

Debased, the town of Stutengarten.
No poet. Nobody at the violin.
Prurient and glistening the day.
Graves, where rotund rats are waiting,
and sounds of dancing feet in ev'ry house of lust.

I draw my circles wide.
Moss crowns black my feet.
The rock becomes cathedral.
Left sweet alone, the well,
and cool and sweet an Aeol's harp.

I take my flute. The forest hums.
The moon is glowing silver.
Listen: from the water weeds, as in days gone by,
arises once more the evergreen god, listening.

163

IMMORTAL VERSE

To die but never! Even seven hundred years
were not to stop my song, enchanting child
and mature woman.
Loving, loving. Gathering riches richly.
The heart a bird, ready to fly within your bosom.

Woman matured. Black tinted brows.
'Tis human wanting to seem better than we are.
The years, mercilessly, like talons of a winged beast
tear away what lovingly once was compared to appleblossom snow.

"Le Parfum pale de la nuit me perce."
Hair falls profusely. "Give me the fencer's verses
and I shall not desire a man to disentangle
my soul during this long night."
She reads, and listens to a whirring sound,
trapped insect dedicated to Our Lady.
My dead heart silently smiles in her mouth.

LAWRENCE SCHECHTERMAN

FRIDAY NIGHT

Agony befalls me again,
My life is a useless wasteland.
With each coming and each going
Repetition dulls my matter.
If only one, one soul,
Would extend a hand, a thought?
Oh cruel, evil, merciless dream,
Throw-up your ugliness,
Relieve this despair!
Repair this infliction,
Which you have set upon me.
Alone: What is it? A word
A thought, or perhaps a memory?
To me it is that summary
Of heartaches and pain,
Which I have had to endure.
Is there nothing in this world for me?
Help! Please someone help me . . .
The night remains silent,
As I expected, as I knew.
No voice stirs the still night air;
I succumb . . . I accept!

164

TIME AND AGAIN

Can it be Autumn,
When Spring has just begun?
Paths are gray,
Yet distant crevices,
With azure-blue approaching.
Normlessness has appeared,
Vanishing hopes surrounded.
Life has ascended,
Ever so minutely,
Should I be aghast?
Let sleep judge fair,
Another interval soon comes.

THE SUBWAY

So arrogant they seem,
Those who force their way,
Through these abundant sphinxes.
Time, more time, so important,
Halts its mighty hand,
As those who pass these portals,
Must forego those passing hands.
Those who stand in such fashion,
Do so not to tarry;
But to find those others,
Who walk with close drapes,
Wrapped 'round the soft and white.
I too, am guilty of these trivials,
But oh! what fond bliss.

M. E. SCHNUR

THE DAWNING

The sun rises slowly
shedding lightening rays
on night's haze fading and
falling before its all powerful
penetrating attack! It falls
defeated.

WINTER WARMTH

White domes from cold the blooms protect
 While through transparent sheets reflect
Warmth of an internal breathing being
 Who must needs the cold deflect.

Wall-less structures aloft on poles
 Protruding bleakly from the soil
With no creature for them to hold
 For winter's warmth is very cold.

White clothes the land mass grey
 Hiding pools of mud underlying all
As fires heat the air and clay
 Frozen heat that does not thaw.

Whisper arms as cold breath touches
 empty limbs exposed to winter
Whose freakish plan makes us suffer so
 many months of ignorant torture?

UNITY IN GREY MINOR

It is grey.
Willows bend as
March breath cruelly
contorts and bends back
supple shivering arms.

The horizon
Also grey sharing
Foggy properties of
objects frayed by distance
and water and day. They are
one, water, fog, and day.

Water dashed
with stormy white
caps atop turbulent
wind-whipped waves only to
come upon stone and fade into
calm water, then recede to the
stubborn sea, helplessly.

Grey is one.
Frenzied excitement
pervades the frozen air.
Kissed by snow eroding stone
traversed in isolation pushed on
by cold, blowing, breathlessness into
a grey horizon. Day is grey, this one.

166

JAMES SCLATER

THE QUESTION

I asked my love why . . .
Why do we convene upon each other's
Thoughts, feelings? We sat probing,
Helplessly searching in vain for the
Answer which would make love supposedly
Easier.

As we pondered, she turned to me with eyes sparkling
And said, "Listen," and touched my cheek
With a deafening roar of silent
Answers.

JUDITH SERIN

THREE POEMS

When the human being argues,
The minutes pause in their circular course
And gather about to watch,
As curling adverbs slash
Or heavy nouns pound noisily.
Time, the oldest animal,
Stares idiot-like
To see a creature fight with wavers of the air,
Rather than teeth and claws.

But the mechanical man-clock in the corner
Obliviously chatters its artificial sentences.

This room, never having contained you,
Is empty, hungry for some remembered smile.
The unexpectant air lies flat, and I am lonely,
Finding no friendliness or opening here.
This room, ignorant, can never know me,
For I am too full with the knowledge of you.
And past-less, this room is dumb and deaf;
It cannot speak to me, nor hear my wordless murmur.
Yet my thoughts have borne you children,
Who wander aimlessly. And, shaking out a blanket,
I hear the rustle of a dream.

Do I see in you
The vulnerability of sumac leaves?
Is that my source of sorrow
While you sleep?
But no. You are protected
From the wind,
It is I who must wander
Among despondent trees.
You are closed-tight,
An entity;
I mingle with the atmosphere,
Subject to impression, injury,
And change of season.
So I am jealous of sleep's
Self-sufficient strength.
Wake, and comfort me
With your incompleteness.

JAMES BARRY SILVER

DRESSED UP MINDS

It seems as though reality
Is absent in my hometown
Eight million people
Are scared to go naked,
To take their masks off
To take their clothes off
— Their fake eyelashes
— Their wigs
— Their contact lenses
— Their defense mechanisms
What do you see?
You ask what I see,
I see nakedness, harshness and cold
I see America as it is
Naked and bare beings
Growing; — outwardly — To escape themselves.

ALAN B. SNYDER

THE HERITAGE OF THE LEMMING

The Moon rises in the West — lifeless Moon!
Pioneer and mechta: all too soon.
Tycho spreads his rays both far and wide —
Alpha, beta, and gamma: all beside.

168

Mother Sun shines bright — ultimate grave!
Savants look to her, the path to pave.
H to helium, the eternal cycle goes.
Ah! All the potency it shows.

To mankind on Earth with all his brains,
Fighting to equal the force. He attains
The Sun's stark strength as he strives to shower
Strontium 90 on each great Power.

On this morning, as the Sun wary spies,
Buttons are pushed — they blot out the skies.
In fields and in forests, all soon die.
To be? Nay! *Not to be* is what they cry.

I look up, and see in the sky
A moving streak — it's Samos the spy.
And then I note a flash like thunder:
A mushroom cloud — world torn asunder.

Now mankind knows that the time has come,
And each man halts as his being grows numb.
Harken to th' eternal voice from deep:
Wake up! It's time to go to sleep!

RICHARD C. SNYDER

FOUND

The thick wooded forest touched the depths of darkness
And each branch reached to the arms of another,
Intertwined
                    but never
Bonded.
The nourishing sunlight found only the aged
And only the aged felt warmth and comfort.

But amidst this confusing complex of bark
The soil gave birth to two pitiful babes,
Unprotected
                    but never
Unarmed.
Their roads of life were mapped from the start,
For only the strongest felt warmth and comfort.

169

Time passed quickly and growth came easily
For the Goal was a process inherent in bodies,
Unchanged
                but never
Doubted.
The drive for height seemed their only ambition,
For only the tallest felt warmth and comfort.

But the hardened bark above now seemed impenetrable
And the taller trees peered down on the two weaker children,
Unwanted
                but never
Alone.
Their infinity of parents scorned and ridiculed them,
For only the bravest felt warmth and comfort.

Soon their branches accepted each other — a union had formed
For there was no place to grow but in each others arms,
Uncontrolled
                but never
Refused.
And each felt its own strength plus the strength of the other,
For only the needed felt warmth and comfort.

R. ERIC STALEY

THE TRAIN STATION

The train station — home of the bum.
A bench for a bed, light for warmth,
Each other as comfort to the misery they share
In a lonely town — they come.

A passing man stops, looks in, moves on.
Faces walk by, purposely ignoring
The old one, the young one, the one snoring;
A stolen glance and their dignity is gone.

An old man ambles from waste can to garbage,
A bent neck, bent back, face bent with sorrow,
Looking for a meal; waiting for tomorrow.
Anxiously rushing to the unwritten page.

A massive moustache stares at a newspaper.
Crumpled, torn, filled with a void of meaning.
His hands shaking what his eyes are cleaning,
Hypnotized by this black and white acre.

170

He in the corner combs his tangled hair
Trying to regain the pride he has lost
On the road, where it has by fortune been tossed.
Each strand stands on end — the echo of despair.

They are all here — the bums.
They wait, read, sleep, pass on.
New ones replace old ones who in turn replace some
Who have left — who have come.

MEMORIES

A life of bright colors;
Hot, a lurid spectrum.
Burning painfully is my mind
Fueled by my past;
Needless suffering now.
I never could color
Within the line.

JAMES T. STAPLES

THE FIRST RAIN

Tear-pressed and ever swelling pools . . .
    first one, then two . . . then showers
So gently wash the parched and crusting face
    of Earth and all within her keep.
Blithe, aromatic airs take flight
    from crevices and pores of shale
Where rivulets explore and seep,
    then sweetly quench an acrid, burning thirst.
Once dusty-green of blade and wilting limb,
    exposed and bathed o'er all . . .
She smartly dons a lacy-green attire
    and breathes a richer, purer, fresher air.
Embellished, cleansed and shining new,
    she smiles a golden smile's delight,
As flashing rays of sun subdue
    the sweeping flow of image-dancing streams.

171

WINTER TAPESTRY

Through frost-tinged air and pearl blue haze
A sway of ghostly art-forms sweeps
Across a span of pine and pond,
Then gently settles, chilled in silent sleep.
From skies of void and arctic gray it comes;
A cloud of speckled lace which dons
Each naked limb and paling blade
In downy vestments primed by winter's wand.
Thus, nature's magic so transforms
A world of waning green and creeping brown
To mystic realms of powdered white,
Where softened shadows shape a season's crown.

JANE STATLANDER

TO ALLEN GINSBURG, MY GURU GOD

You, Guru god
Have charmed out the reams of crazy reason
From the freaky patterned parlors of my brain.
You are a brave psychedelic knight
In an endless day of loud bleating suns
Which pierce my head inward
To the inside of this implosion which I can only call "me".
Can I travel along
The muscled streets and bloody roads
Of my arms,
My face,
My neck,
My pussy-
Cat heart
To find the nitty-gritty "me"?
The "me" of all
Those hotted-up snapshots of dimply babies;
The "me" of pictures with anonymous
Chicken soup aunts with arthritic fingers
And fat bullied dickless uncles;
The "me" of the pictures with small cousins
Who already seemed to know the mean justices
Of their lives to come.

My fierce day is an endless time
Of dreamless dreams
Of subdivided "me's";

172

Of scorching faces
Transfixing with synthetic grins
Which interrupt my holy flight with you
Atop some wild horse;
(Or shall we hop a ride on a canni-
Bus leaving for Freak-out?)

Is it too late?
Can I hide from this fake day
Of self-capsulated chatter
And a myriad of social intro-

Douches before my soul goes through its
Asphalt menopause
And spills no more its delirious
Fantastic blood upon this crazy earth.

JEFF STEARNS

Four nuns
          stepping
                    along the beach
          dressed in black
One scuttles through
          the ocean's backflow to be

                              alone

She grasps
          a shell

                                        deserted

          by a creature or
                    separated by the
                              commanding
                                        waves

Look!
          the shell
          lively colors

                              yellow, red, green
                    it makes me
                              want to dance
                    and to love . . .

173

LAURENCE STEPHENS

THE FAMOUS SIGN

Impossibilium nulla obligatio est.
Corpus Iuris Civilis.

The jowly man with bright new teeth
Extends a ringed and palsied hand
To stop the youth who walks beneath
The faded awnings of the Strand.

The pigeons overhead on wires
Watch forgotten buried gods
Below the street tilt churches' spires
And cautious Hesiod play the odds.

Cato-like the old man tells
The story of the aged priest
Who no longer rings his bells
But listens only at the East.

While in doorways Hermes leans,
God of theft and boundary line,
Straining now for what he means
And holding out his famous sign.

LINDA JO STERN

DIEM SIN FOO, HOW'S BY YOU?

Diem Sin Foo will marry you Madame LeFarge.
Your finger is swollen and large from
so much knitting and sitting but
No quitting. Oh no. Not you.
        God forbid. it's morbid.
The Hung Shoo Gai will never die.
If it does it will be a sulplise to all.
So tall. and blond? Bond? Yes.
007; he went to heaven and
baked bread with leaven(ing)
Sing! Sing!
About a ring. around.
No sound. but mounds and mounds
Peter and Paul oh but Mary
is not contrary. Not hairy
        but be wary.

174

Sarie. a daughter will not
Slaughter who wrote a book.
Look! Life! What a strife.
Knife the loafmeat and watch the pourdown
Eat the clown.
Such a lot of fuzz. Buzz.
A friend from Shaker.
Make her a chair shop.
Stop!!
Please? on her knees.
in the bees behind the trees
and the breeze.
How loverleeze.

FOREVER

When the ends of a rabbit's ears touch the twinkle of a star.
Where the door of a groundhog's home leads.
Where the edge of a pin points.
The depth of a toybox.
The life of a good book.
Time.
A memory.
My love for you.

ESTHER GRADY STONE

EN ROUTE

Brume du matin sur la rivière,
Se levant vers les cimes des monts,
Adoucit au réveil l'atmosphère rosée.

Rayons du soleil faible, brillant tamisés à travers les vapeurs,
Eclaircissent un endroit
Caché entre les hautes collines.

L'écume blanche de l'eau turbulente
Se heurte, riant,
Contre les rochers mornes à mi-courant.

Les forêts épaisses, montant jusqu'au ciel,
Majestueuses devant la mort,
Commencent à se colorer en rouge, orange, et jaune.

Du chemin étroit, ciselé entre les murailles
D'argile et d'ardoise, escarpées et raides,
L'oeil plonge dans le vallon endormi.

Il apercoit un vieux pont en bois
El quelques petites maisonnettes
Perchées sur une côte.

Sous un ciel gris-bleu . . . le silence règne
Pas un cri d'oiseau au fraîcheur du petit jour . . .
La solitude . . . le calme . . .

C'est un paysage délicieux qui me fait oublier . . .
Qui me fait sentir la paix
Dans tout mon être.

WM. F. STOUT

i sit in a cemetery
and wonder about truth.

the truth of the writhing belly
of a snake

the truth of the purity of a hitler's soul

the truth of the hindu ascetic
whose legs atrophied from sitting
in the same lotus position
for twenty years

the truth of mothers' milk squirting

the truth of mr jesus christ hanging on a tree
and mr ferlinghetti making a hippy poem about it

the truth of myself lying on a bed looking
at a wet-stone grey buddha through mists of incense
colored red by burning vigil lights stolen
late one night from a catholic church

the truth of madness in a small room
reading genet celine sade
listening to a requiem

the truth of being drunk on wine
high on pot
delirious on cunt
insane on everything
hopelessly miserably insane

176

DONNA SWAN

A TREE IS GONE

She stood so straight and tall in fertile Spring,
Her small ones tender grew in sandy soil.
From blushing blossoms bluest birds did sing,
Of future golden harvest without toil.
My salty tears by summer rains were spilled.
Her blossoms withered in the summer moon.
Her simple grave with shriveled flowers filled,
Her barren frame fell broken much too soon.
The Heaven's wolves howl their loud lament,
When winter's wind too early chills green fruits,
Or those whose usefulness is not yet spent.
We live, survive, but half without our roots.
My heart in broken pieces pricks my breast
With pain. Since you were called in youth to rest.

ROSEMARY SWAN

DURATION

Enduring
  Lasting
    Love
Existed for me in your
Tender,
  Caressing
    Arms.

Exquisite,
  Beautiful
    Peace
Was to be found only in your
Calming,
  Silencing
    Lips.

Then you died.

Agonizing,
  Painful
    Memories
Were engraved in my
Confused,
  Grieving
    Mind.

```
          Deathless,
            Incessant
               Loneliness
          Was the price of my
          Rapturous,
             Devoted
                Life.
```

ARTHUR S. TAMKIN

THE NIGHT

Quickly came the night.
Engulfed in darkness
And twirling into murky mist,
I lost your hand.

Yet just before
We saw the daylight sun.
We basked in its warm rays,
And walked apace.

Our plans were bold.
Our vision was a banner,
unfurled and strong.
We dared to hope.

And now you are not here.
The night has come,
And immersed in darkness,
I walk alone.

NICK TATRO

NO AMERICA

i'm not going america
my oozing gore won't salve your acned face
my Death won't cure your gold perverted race

don't expect me to get a hard-on about your War
just cause you've got your hand on asia's thigh
there are other rice bowls for me america

no thanks again america i know your taste in women
remember, i nearly drowned in your
Bay of Pigs before

LA FLORIDE

Sitting in her orange-scented bubble bath
Mother dreams of Florida
Of childhood in Rose Cottage
Above the hollow and the Negro church
Where she still plays enraptured by Spring
                              and Orange blossoms
She dreams of orchard-delights of ready-made
                              desserts
Of Moonlight strolls in neatly ordered groves
And Nectarine kisses by Tangerine trees

Dreaming of Florida
And hordes of Mandarins under chairs
While purging city air
With a lemon tart reprimand from an aerosal can

She dreams of a picker Zeke
Whose frosted black frame bent under the
Sweet-smelling baskets of fruit
And who died in the shed all tired and lame

Mother worships the Temple orange
Tangelos hang from her ears
She plants citrus box gardens on the 30th
Floor of her Chicago tenement

Mother let a grapefruit rot under the front seat of her car
And now the rank scent and the gruesome white mould

    Rot her dream world green world
    And dirty her bubble bath
    Mother lives in the citric
    Mist of the past;
    Mother is dying.

PETER THOMAS

AND LACE

One faint candle glimmer whispers,
Lisping delicate syllables
Like feathers slowly weighing down
My eyelids; softly weighing down as
I silent strain for its whispered
Secrets. At the window, feather
Frost and lace, but wool inside. The
Stars winking, nodding off to sleep.

BY WIND, NETTED

The wind brushed softly toward the mountains,
wind brushing the plain, burnishing dried fields,
wind brushing past him as he returned, toward the hills,
wandering from the home he did not know,
wind brushing eastward,
lacing him to itself.
Clouds flowed in the river of wind,
flowing eastward toward the mountains, flowing above him,
his steps scarring the ripening grain.
Clouds tossing like stallions of many tones
of grey, tossing like chunks of ice in a bone chill stream,
tossing like wind-angered seas,
tossing like blue white smoke tumbling upward from a
    gutted house,
clouds tossing him eastward.
The sun behind him glowing, a clouded golden light that
drizzled through the clouds,
light sinking into the clouds and gone.
The plain losing burnished gold, dulling, now a withered brown,
his steps slashing a dark scar across the withered plain,
the boy smelling the dust of the plain,
smelling the snow in the clouds.
The child wandering eastward with the wind,
the wind gusting against the mountain walls,
drifting snow crystals against the stone walls of the hills,
snow flicking grey and white in the air
snow lacing against the mountains
scarring the stone.
Snow stinging from the clouds, dancing in the blowing wind,
knifing into the grain not harvested, bone chill
snow, wind lacing into him
lacing him to itself.
Ice clutching to the banks of the river of wind,
ice clogging the river, icing the river,
Lethe ending the day,
ending the tossed contorted greys of sky,
Lethe ending the day, ending the night, ending the storm.
Snow stinging the boy as he wandered eastward,
snow filling the scars of the plain,
icing the frostbitten browns, icing the greys,
as the boy cowered from the wind, clinging close to the earth,
the red earth,
the earth now cold and dried,
the red earth scarred with his steps,
while the wind blasted eastward,
lacing him to itself.

SAND DUNE: SUMMER

The sky, sun seared, arches above me as
I trace ideas in the lines of driftwood,
Sifting sand into rotted knotholes,
Dispersing it with my breath. Holding up
The sky — giant log pillars, scarred and smoothed
By wind sweeping the sand; my
Right hand on one and my left on the
Other, I stand watching the play of light on
The sand, the dance of leaves in the wind,
Watching the trees stretch in the wind.
I run to the old dead birch, its bark-covered
Branches a vast net to catch the sky,
And marvel at this snow in summer.
Snow: crystalled whiteness
Glittering under an ancient, amber light.

ALLEN TILLEY

COMMUNICATIONS

Dirges sounding (dreary,
you must guess, never having heard,
passing the dead in silence)
wail out the evening.
Affirmation ushers always.

Clumsy feelings sounding foreign
trumpeting humbling kinship's might;
wonder in remembered daylight,
jostle in must tender night.
Can if reaching tendril outward
hear a comeback wayworn whisper:
can if never, arching outward,
throw an image.

ANTICIPATION OF CLIMAX

Should I lie death ridden, magically bereft
of pain that conscious moments project on death,
morphine shot strive to throw words
to placate the jaws of my final fate
my last thought, bubble burst, if given time
to ponder would muddle up my throat for release.
It might be damn near in the brookbed early morning.

181

TO OFFSPRING

You come to an old world, worn by my ways;
rocks, that were individual artifices, fuse
and fret in grown ancient anonymity.
Words once a charged fire
holding all that brim-burst thought
grow weary, veer and float in feather dusk.
You in your quickening intricacy
see to discover what now is known.
The final fruition has heaved
its barely breathed truth flat to the stars.

A CONVERSION

"Take up thy cross and follow me."
I heard — so pungent, so compelling
That charged with finest fire I rushed
To bear all, to scrape the flesh
From my hands on the rough wood, to tear
Painfully the hewn cross from the ground,
Heft it and trudge gloriously to heaven.
I grasped the surface surprisingly slick
Of a ponderous looking cross, pulled mightily
And uprooted the hollow thing.
I watched it bounce on the ground,
Listened to the jeers of a growing crowd,
Turned red, turned away, and ran
To ponder my defeat at the hands
Of a sham cross. I re-gathered myself
For a second assault. I searched long,
Swollen-footed and panting came I
At finality to the challenge, a monolith
Of a cross, surmounting high hill
And topping taller tree. Gigantic it loomed,
Magnificent it seemed, gargantuan in prospect.
I strode to the living cross, straddled it,
Enfolded it in my arms, tensed and heaved. Then
Were many mighty man-days, longmuscle spent in toil
And groaning. At length it came to be
That the cross in my arms became a tree.
Grandeur of form dissolved to leafy profusion
And I collapsed with a horrible sickness.
Long did I lie there.
I arose at last with a mighty shiver
And rending sigh, shouldered my defeat
And carried it to Him.

THEODORE N. TRIKILIS

Love, you old dog,
  you've stolen
    my heart
      as a bone,

And buried it
  beneath a pile
    of forgotten dreams,

A huge hole dug deep
  into Time's backyard,

To tenderize it,
  To hide its scars,
    To save it for another day.

THE FOOL

So I am but a fool!
  Yes, maybe it is so,
The truth has a funny way of exposing itself,
  But perchance there be a place for such as I,
A quiet lonely island in the middle of a lost idea,
 A planet bound out into the deep endless space of everlasting Hope,
  A tomb buried beneath a pile of forgotten dreams,
    A step just one step beyond Infinity,
      And being located in one of these regions, one
        may ask of time,
      "How long will it take to get there?"

  How long is a dream, an idea, a ray of Hope?
    How far is Infinity?
The answer can only be estimated with a reference to Eternity,
  And being thus, I can say it is only as long as the faith
    You have in what you believe —
      Be your belief in buttons, in cows, in money, in apples,
    Or perhaps, in God,
      It really matters not,
    Only if the belief is strong and true,

So I believe in buttons and you say I am a fool.

HERE

Here I sit, thinking about being There,
    Heretofore I was content with Here,
        Herein I shall struggle to be There,
            Hereabout I found solitude,
                Hereafter I shall search for the meaning of There,
                Hereof There shall give me the answer,
                Herewith I shall be puzzled no more,
            Hereupon Life will have a new meaning within me,
        Hereby giving me strength to succeed,
And There I shall stand.

TODAY, YESTERDAY, TOMORROW

Here is a soul without desire,
Here is a man without a purpose in life,
Here is a fool,
Like a plant, he wants nothing, expects nothing,
    Life without dreams,
        A soul without a tomorrow,
            A fool with only yesterdays,
                Only a memory of a life he would have had,
Happiness is only a frame of mind,
    Loneliness is a condition of the body and the mind together.
        Today I live,
        Yesterday I loved,
        Tomorrow I will die,
            My life is but three days,
                But being only three days, I find that Tomorrow will
                last only a fraction of a second,
                    Today lasts only a fraction of a minute,
                        Yesterday lasted an Eternity.
And having lasted an Eternity, I can say that I truly lived a
fruitful life,
        One of everlasting love.

BARRI TUCKER

DON'T LEAVE

Don't leave,
now is the time to begin, please
        don't leave
with our moments then
and all that we've spent together
        dear Angelo,

184

angel wings of winter children
crucified beneath some trash can man
who was only doing his job
poor Angelo.
O I suppose
they'll find another drift
the snow will come again
and angels live.

             Don't leave
with me this our yesterday
now is the time
just once let me find today
or love even
I've seen
in every naked canvas colored
and blue notes
             don't leave
now is the time
now Angelo

DAN TULLY

VIET NAM

Sick
shit
red curds
agāpe
with eyes

             phallic
             nasal projections
             creamy
             white death

                          figs
                          compūsing
                          philsophisters
                          Gowd!

MELINDA VADAS

THE WAY DOWN

Tomorrow is bleak;
I've passed the peak.
I'm on the way down:
Nowhere is my hometown.
My problem, be it great or small
Is that I've never been up at all.

THE PURPLE SKY

I say the sky is of a purple hue;
Upon this I stake my life.
You say the sky is blue, others agree with you.
Must I lose my life?
The sky is no less purple to me
Because of the blue that others see.

MARION WALSH

TWO POEMS

Quiet forest sounds
haunt the grey twisted trees
which blend with sighing winds
and whisper universal secrets
to the breathing earth.

Locust birds emit sonic sounds of secret knowledge,
worshipping in ancient wisdom
the solar eye of the world,
and life is continuous
and wordless
possessing one great Intelligence.

A leaf falls from up somewhere —
an invitation to Eternity,
and loses itself in the wind
until suspended in a fine mist of web.

Christ mournfully passes a dying child on the steps,
and loses himself in the rain,
Dissolving into fragments
of scattered dream reality.

186

City buildings hung from clouds,
People swarming with weary eyes around them
as soot drifts on gentle wind currents
and settles on their eyelashes
and their noses.

Statues — monuments to unreality,
watch the shifting, floating crowds
of scattered man
pursuing ruin and ecstacy.
The bearded long-haired prophets
stand beside the statues on streetcorners
shouting silently
their ageless messages
with hopeless bloodshot eyes.

The city —
hung-up on clouds
and soot
and empty rooftops,
Unknowingly
adjusts itself to its ruinous fate.

VERNON WARING

DISENCHANTMENT OF THE TIGHTROPE WALKER

Suspending moments
atop this spindle stretch,
the thick thread
tugged tight under
his shifting feet,
his eyes catch
the spotlight
glinting toward ring one.

Mystified by the knife-thrower,
he is strangely thrown,
hands leaping endlessly
through a somersault sky;
hands to head, hands to chest,
then to thigh while
knives turn quickly
and a liquored mob shouts;
their voices breaking
against the freakshow tent.

187

RICHARD WATTS

ALLEN GINSBERG
Dedicated to Frank Wolf

Where fungus fails to grow
patches of flesh appear:
the peak of a nose
pink isletic lips
. . . two eyes submerged under glass.
He is an old indian chanting
an I.B.M. machine freed to think
. . . pheasant under glass.
He is a recorder, recording sounds
sounds recorded for your ear and mine
sounds we ourselves fail to hear;
yesterday I listened to recording sounds,
to someone sitting on the pot and burping
I was shocked
but worse yet
failed to recognise me.

THE PRISON MAKER

Everyday there was chattering gossip, but nothing said
Chattering, chattering, chattering!
I had to retreat behind my newspaper
and even then the thundering, changing of the underground
   reached me
and moved my indifference to anger.
It was then that I viewed my reflection in the glass
and peeked through the bars
at the brick and stone opposite me;
I was a prisoner within.
I could not escape
the ghostly haunted echo
of the prison steps.
Stone upon stone down Piccadilly
I begged for my freedom
but the brushed, rushed indifference of the streets
only hypnotized me to the river
and Big Ben towered over me like a prison guard
and no one listened to me, but the river Thames
and the river listened eternally.

188

His broken lips suckled the spiral tit of burgundy
while his bottom covered patted paper—yesterday's padded news
and he coiling in the vertigo of love was found
broke like a broken slot machine
but found never-the-less making love
with a woman half his age.
He sat twelve yards from her
and they embraced,
he behind a wooden fence
and she behind an open window;
daily through a hole in the wood
her raisin tits were suckled by his broken lips
and by the clock's loving melody they embraced
for she undresses, re-dresses and un-re-dresses
on the hour every hour
always near a shadeless window.

THE THIRD PART OF A LOVE TRILOGY
Dedicated to Judy Walker

the train moves like a timid boy
its whistle babbles in the night
its pale smoke becomes a vessel in the sky
in the seat next to me someone cries
and my love
with sanguine cheeks
stands under the sheltered platform.
The crystal pygmies dance their funeral rite
upon my face
the dark sorrowful trees
rush past
and as the sheltered platform
shrinks
I grip my love's handkerchief.

LOVE'S THE RUB OF DRUNKENNESS AND SUICIDE
Dedicated to Miss Alison Yoder

Love's the rub of drunkenness and suicide
of ringing madness and mourning dress
of holding hands and softly laughing through your tears.
And lovers are quiet magicians in a child's theatre
and out of the hat poetry they recite
and music is the merging of wheels on pavement.
But, suddenly, the children are adults

189

the show closes down
and the magicians lose their magic and separate;
the wheels on pavement vanish into everyday sounds,
and poetry is put back into books,
for the ringing madness and drunkenness are gone
and they are sober and sane and suicide
never enters their brains.

BREATHLESS AMERICA
Dedicated to Yevgeny Yevtushenko

In moments to come we will possess the hammer
and the hammer possessing us will strike again and again:
Damn! Damn! Damn!
We will carve Siamese twins out of our late Lady's torch
and the poet will be part of the 'brotherhood';
like us he won't want, for bed and bread,
like us he will be part of the Greek chorus.
We, the sickle, will cut every daffodil in two
we, the Sun, will erase every single star
we, the octopus, will exterminate the eagle in flight
and since our coming the eye has become extinct.

LESLIE B. WHITBECK

I WATCH THE MANY

I watch the many
I watch them go
I've cared for any
And I know.

Don't look down
Don't look down
Tiny ants
Are on the ground
Always lost
Never found.

Blue sky dark earth
Mildred mildred giving birth
Stoops her young
In other's dung
And bellows empty
One more cow.

190

William William wake up now
Mourning's morning
Grandpa died
Grandma's dead
Mother cries
And holds her head
Stand up straight November day
Lift a casket just this way
Grey against the pit
Shovel shovel over it
They cover child grandpa's play.

In love with love
Dim night's sight
Of first white breast
The dizzy height
Of first time love
And well deep lost
Of a new fount
Lonely in the separate comings
Going in the headlights home
Alone.

I watch the many
I watch them go
I've cared for any
And I know.

MARILYN WHITE

ECCLESIASTICAL ECLIPSE

Balanced on a precipice,
One foot with land its rank,
The other claiming as its own
Air's mystic covenant.

Harmony endures not long;
Soon both must choose but one:
Mortal land, immortal air,
Lucidity or plunge?

I live with what I know, the land;
In air one chances fraud.
Yet anguish plagues,
For can one be
A saint without a God?

BRUCE WINGO

THE CITY

and where are the trees so tall
and the leaves that fall with autumn
and the grass so green and fresh
and the birds of the sky so free
and all the other tails i've heard
around concrete walls
and through the asphalt vines

and there is a city forest
where trees grow tall
and are concrete and steel
and climb to the sky
and blot out the sun's rays
and neon signs show the way for travellers

and the people are made of concrete
and souls of asphalt
and hearts of steel
and they are feared like animals
that roam the jungles
and they lurk in alley ways
and hide in back streets
and wait

and i prefer the streams
and tiny brooks
and the green fields
and a place where each dawn is new
and where birds sing in the silence
of a new sundown

GERRY A. WOLFF

A TONAL POEM

The Sea is up
The Sea is down
The Sea is all around
The Sea is you
The Sea is me
The Sea is us

192

The Sea is froth
The Sea is foam
The Sea is home
The Sea is gloom
    The Sea churls and spills
    The Sea hurts and kills
    The Sea warms and chills
    The Sea pounds on
        Rushing, raving,
        Endlessly craving,
        The Sea pushes on

The Sea stilling, comforting
The Sea ravaging, plummeting
The Sea beckoning, echoing
The Sea conquers —
        In the end the Sea
        Is all that remains
        We have returned all
        To its rightful place
The Sea is you
    The Sea is me
        The Sea is us

YEVGENII YEVTUSHENKO

Translated by Paul J. Cassidy

AN INCANTATION

Some night in spring think of me
And think on a summer night of me.
Some fall night think of me
And think some winter's night of me.
Even if I'm not there with you but somewhere free,
As far away as in another century,
On the long, cool sheet lie easily,
As if floating on your back upon the sea,
Yielding to a soft wave rolling languidly,
In private with me alone, as with the sea.

I wouldn't have you think of me by day.
Let day invert your world and then straightaway
Flood you with its fumes and its wine's bouquet,
Expelling thoughts of me, driving them astray.
You may think of what you please — while it's day,
But at night think only of me, I pray.

Listen and hear through the whistle of the train,
Through the wind that shreds the clouds like a hurricane,
How I — in misfortune's tangled skein —
Want you, in your room so small and plain,
To shut your eyes for joy with an anguished strain,
Pressing palms against temples till you feel the pain.

I beg of you: when all is hushed tranquillity,
Or when the rain up above roars noisily,
Or when the snow at your window glistens silvery,
Asleep yet not asleep, floating drowsily —
Some night in spring think of me
And think on a summer night of me.
Some fall night think of me
And think some winter's night of me.

WHEN LIKE THE MOON YOUR FACE AROSE . . .

When like the moon your face arose
Above this crumpled life of mine,
At first I only realized
How meagre was all that I possessed.
But on the rivers, groves, and seas
You shed that special light of yours,
And into the colours of the world
Led uninitiated me.
O how I dread, O how I dread
This unexpected moon's decline,
An end to discovery, tears, delight;
But I do not combat this fear.
I understand: This fear of mine
Is love itself. I cherish it,
Though indeed I know not how,
I, love's neglectful guardian.
This fear has caught me and ensnared me.
Such moments as these — I know — are brief,
And for me all colours will fade and vanish
When like the moon you sink and set.

194

ANTHONY ORIN YOUNG

TIMMY CHRISTOPHER LIKED TO PLAY GOD

Timmy Christopher liked to play God;
His parents thought that odd.
"But it's been done before!" he would explain.
Say daddy, "I think that boy's insane."
"Well just you watch!" as he opened a hatch
And chased some ants with a lighted match.
"See, I'm God, " said Timmy brightly.
His mother thought such behavior unsightly.
She say, "come, come young fool! 'Tis Sunday morn
we must scurry off to church to avoid His scorn."
"I'm no ant," sayeth Timmy.

THOUGHTS THAT TRICKLE FROM THEE THIGH

Imagine, if you will, Chief Sitting Bull.
      Oh, he's so good.
You say you've never met him?
      We soon will fix that straight.
You never will forget him.
      He'll be your groovy mate!
He's got the wildest teeth,
      Never had a fillin'
He stays away from the sacred stones,
      But he swims inside Mr. Dylan.

                  He's carrots peeled,
                        tomato juice,
                        tobasco sauce,
                              and love turned lose.

            So smooth and loving, loving, loving all the
                                                    time.

195

M. H. ZIMMERMAN

PHYSICAL IDENTITY

I see myself jumping up and down
In a crowded, old, well-used gym,
And breathing out while descending
And inhaling on the upsurge.

I hear *my* breathing;
I feel *my* muscles tense;

And I look up and see everybody

else

Jumping up and down.